HERO

Mastering The 17 Spiritual Stages

M. A. Stephenson

ISBN: 0692909966
ISBN 13: 9780692909966

DEDICATION

For those who started out on the journey to greatness,
But met with trials and difficulties, have yet to succeed,
Or worse yet, gave up entirely,
For those stuck in bondage to addiction,
Unable to overcome temptation,
For those frustrated with reality as it is,
I present a road map,
By which you may find yourself again on the path of life,
And doing so,
Right yourself, and achieve victory and fulfillment,
Interpreted and applied to daily life,
For the first time ever,
In one volume,
Hero: Mastering The 17 Spiritual Stages

TABLE OF CONTENTS

Introduction   vii

Act One   1
1   Call to Adventure   5
2   Refusal of the Call   12
3   Supernatural Aid   20
4   Crossing of the First Threshold   28
5   Belly of the Whale   36

Act Two   41
6   The Road of Trials   47
7   Meeting with the Goddess   55
8   Woman as Temptress   63
9   Atonement with the Father   73
10   Apotheosis   84
11   Ultimate Boon   91

Act Three   97
12   Refusal of the Return   103
13   Magic Flight   109

14   Rescue from Without   117
15   The Crossing of the Return Threshold   124
16   Master of the Two Worlds   130
17   Freedom to Live   137

Conclusion   145
Final Benediction   148
Appendix A—Example Journey   150
Appendix B—Inventory of Gifts   154
Appendix C—Exercises   156
Bibliography   162

INTRODUCTION

The following work is a distillation of timeless wisdom from symbolic imagery into nonsymbolic language. It is meant to be clear and easy to understand. It leans on the groundwork laid by Joseph Campbell in his work *The Hero with a Thousand Faces* and on the worldwide myths and legends that have permeated the human consciousness.

I am not attempting to put forth any new perspective. The ideas contained in this book are not my own conjecture or reasoning. Instead, they are the synthesized and compacted views of centuries of storytellers and wise men and women, presented in a form that ought to be easy to understand and apply to daily life.

Understanding the Following Journey

The journey contained in this book moves through several distinct stages. It is a journey of transformation – a journey in which you will set out to accomplish some great outward dream or vision. It is also one on which you will find yourself diving deeply into hidden realms of your own mind. It is a mystical journey, an adventure meant to lead you on a path to accomplish your destiny and embody the hero you were born to become.

In the pages of this book, you will find hidden wisdom from ages past. This wisdom will be unlocked before your eyes. It will reveal to you the road you must travel to fulfill your dreams. It will show you how to become truly great. This book answers the question of why so few become great in life, and how to overcome the struggles you will face along the way if you attempt to do so.

The ancients knew and appreciated what it took to be truly heroic. The stories they told hold the keys to completing the greatest quest known to man—achieving your destiny, fulfilling your dream, living your true life calling. The way they told of was not always easy—but it was real. Though told through image and story, the underlying meaning of their words hold great significance. In them we discover keys for understanding our own humanity. We learn of our place in the world, and how to overcome the various challenges life sends our way. If you wish to fulfill your own dream, I encourage you to read this book in its entirety. While at times it may challenge you, the challenge will be far less than the trials life presents to you along the way.

It is my hope that this book will prepare you with the mindsets and understanding to break free from the norm and change the world. By engaging with images presented, you will learn, grow, and transform. By the time you are finished you will hold a newfound mastery of the world in your hands.

The Fractals of Life
I know math may not have been your favorite subject, but let's use it here as a metaphor. I think doing so will form the basis

for an enlightening discussion of the journey to come. If this section really bogs you down, I suggest skipping it and turning straight to 'Act One'. The rest of the book isn't quite so dense, and anyone should be able to glean tremendous understanding from its pages.

What follows is not a formula that holds the secret of success in life. Instead, what follows is a succession of formulae that hopes to offer some approximation of the journey we call life. As we all have learned from facing struggles in almost everything we have tried to accomplish, life is not an A + B = C kind of affair. It is not as simple as arithmetic; it refuses to be constrained to the simplicities of elementary mathematics.

If we stop and look at our physical universe, it becomes quite clear, as in physics textbooks, that the mechanical workings of the world can indeed be expressed—in fact, are best expressed—in mathematical terms. The problem for the everyday person is just that the mathematical systems in question are so infinitely complex that they seem beyond the reach of understanding.

The common person seeks to simplify his or her life and make its challenges and hurdles easier to overcome. Unfortunately, with every degree of simplification we apply to a complex formula, the less clarity we achieve in expressing the whole. For example, if we take what is known in basic algebra as a quadratic equation, which when graphed consists of peaks and valleys, and we express it in simple arithmetic terms, dropping out the squares and multiplications so that we are left with only pluses and minuses, then we end with a straight line. As a metaphor for life, that straight line will express none of the valleys and peaks, none of the challenges, only life's general direction. So then, if we end with a line that says, "Life gets better!" we may be surprised that it does so in large advances followed generally by small setbacks.

On the other hand, if we were to look at the original equation on which life was modeled, we would understand at once that, yes, in general, life does get better, but it takes all sorts of twists and turns to get there. And the variables of that quadratic—or, rather, infinitely more complex equation—are centered squarely on our choices and responses to those very peaks and valleys. Which way the equation plays out now takes on an entirely differential expression, determined by so many intrinsic variables of self-expression and free will that suddenly our ability to map such a thing on paper spirals far beyond our control, and we are left with what we can describe only as a "mystery," as "holy" or "good," or as some religious term that leaves the essential processes undefined and returns us immediately to some simple straight line and exhorts us to trust, to have faith.

However, what if there were some middle ground? What if instead of trying to boil the whole thing down to one simple equation, we came away with the desire to write some system of equations? That is, a series of equations that, when taken together, model the entire object in question: life itself. While theoretically it may be impossible to produce just one simple equation due to the grand complexity of the original equation, it may indeed be possible to begin approximating what we call life by creating this sufficiently complex system of equations.

In such a system, each equation may have several variables of its own. The decisions we make at various stages of life and the corresponding factors that produce that specific stage, for example. However, when these equations are taken one after the other, with each individual equation now contributing some understanding of a specific part of the whole, it may begin to reflect the reality of the situation. Although still an approximation instead of a definite expression of the infinitely complex system we call life, it would start to look and feel just a little bit like life itself.

We see the peaks and valleys start to form. In the expression of the individual equations that define essential elements, we can inspect various choices and their effects on the ever-proceeding expression of this life system. The system of equations does not precisely measure the whole. There are still slight turbulences unexpected or undescribed by the equations that push or pull on the graph of life, and these occur because we live in a world full of free-will beings. However, the overarching governing dynamics tend to course-correct when possible and express with a degree of reliability that form we originally found in our system.

A picture starts to form not of a two-dimensional graph but of a three-dimensional shape much like a tree. The equations of the system describe the stem, the branches, and the leaves. They describe the shape, gently modeled. Where in real life the tree may have sharply defined features, this tree-like system of equations we build has only soft curves. Those curves, however, are enough to help us navigate life and can contribute to a vast degree of success we never before could have accessed.

If this is possible, then it would be a very worthwhile goal to pursue. Indeed, coming to an understanding of the interplays of life at a degree that surpasses the knowledge of previous saints and wise men and women would be of vast benefit to our human culture and society.

However, on closer inspection, it appears that the wise men and women of past ages did possess such a system, and to this very day, it surrounds us. We are all intimately familiar with its ways and workings, for they have been ingrained in us since we were children. Unfortunately, just as a thing can be there all along but, until it is clearly identified and explained, go entirely unnoticed, you may not even realize that this system exists.

For it is hidden in plain sight—in the most obvious yet childlike of places—in the myths and metaphors of religions, ancient legends, and everyday stories. It is in the tales of wise men and women of ages past and of modern-day superheroes in equal portion.

This is the hero's journey, what Joseph Campbell describes as the monomyth. Its formulation, as he describes it, consists of seventeen individual stages (or what we may refer to in this discussion as formulae), each with its own set of unique variables and free-will choices to be made. For the purposes of this book, I have kept the titles of the stages exactly as they are in Campbell's original work.

The choices we make in these stages determine the outcome we will receive from the world. It is the goal of this book, then, to make you aware of the stages themselves and clearly define what choices you must make for the best possible outcome.

With the succession of formulae precisely defined, it is then we must realize that although myth and story generally separate these stages into a beautiful play, every single one of the stages is playing itself out every day. These are the threads of the tapestry of life—and every one of them starts at the beginning of the tapestry and works itself all the way through to the end. However, as we become aware of this journey and begin to work through its stages for ourselves, we find, as in storytelling, that at certain times and seasons, individual stages begin to pronounce themselves on the play of life in exaggerated ways.

Returning to the metaphor of mathematical formulae, we may then say that, for the most part, these formulae individually express themselves as some very small value, let's say 0.01 or 0.02. However, we might suddenly arrive to a point in life where an individual formula will resolve a much larger value, for example 10, or 100, or 1,000, thus overshadowing every other formula in the equation.

For some people, one of these formulae will sometimes hold such an incredible value that the individual thinks it is the entirety of the equation, and at once they go and tell everyone they can about their specific element. "If you only could fix this one specific thing," they claim to anyone who will listen, "your life would be perfect!" And for them, that may indeed be their local version of reality. Not only that, but they will likely find some similar souls who deeply need their specific message because it resolves some deep problem specific to that individual.

However, for every individual with whom that formula resonates, countless more will call it rubbish. For them, their own formulae of life have not resolved themselves to require such an emphasis on the one element the self-proclaimed guide now expounds.

So eventually we come to a time in the world in which the number of religions and possible paths seems as vast as the sea. We all glimpse at certain times a seeming magic beneath the noise and confusion, but as the equations of life prove themselves to be infinitely more complex than we had once hoped, we lose faith in the equation altogether—unless we are willing to surrender ourselves to blind faith and believe beyond reason in our one chosen element.

It need not be this way. We can zoom out on the tapestry of life, and instead of harping on one specific element as if it were the whole, we can see the entire picture. Now, in one system of equations we can express an approximation that is sufficiently close to the real thing so as to be of value to daily life.

We no longer need to say, "It's A plus B, and if you don't agree with me, you are wrong!" Instead, we can say, "My current life equation is expressing itself as the following set of seventeen individual equations, each with its own current value."

And while still the mystic or seer might set out to define life as a set of one hundred equations, for the average person, seventeen is likely enough. It is enough to accomplish something great in life, enough to see significant transformation happen. It is enough to allow the journeyman to brave the trials and storms of life with an intelligent appreciation for just what, exactly, is happening right while it happens. In this way he may answer whatever challenge or trial presents itself simply—as if he had the cheat sheet to life—with precisely the right response right away. Having done so, he will then find that he may progress immediately to the next stage (or at least as quickly as that stage will allow, for some stages do require a temporal element that cannot be wished away).

The person who has completed all seventeen stages is the true hero of life, possessing such mastery of all required fields of thought and expression that he or she can relate to nearly all the individual perspectives of life and, being grounded in unselfish love and giving, express kindness to all he or she meets along the way.

ACT ONE

The Ordinary World

I write this book today after many years of personal searching. I am not new to the journey of self-transformation or of healing or spirituality. My journey has been long and varied, but that does not qualify me as an authority on the matter.

What qualifies me is my innate connection to humanity through those genes and molecules of DNA we all hold in common. We are, in the end, all human. We all, no matter religion, sex, or skin tone, have in common the vast majority of our genetic factors.

In addition to those molecules that link us to one another, we also share a common history: the history of our world. Although race and nationality cause those histories to vary to one degree or another, they all exist alongside one another— at times clashing, yet not thereby separated. Collectively, these histories form the basis of myth, and it is from that one common myth, which Joseph Campbell calls the monomyth, that the basis of this work is formed.

The journey of transformation that changes a person into a hero has a beginning, like all good stories do. This beginning, in the three-act structure, is known as starting out or as the ordinary world. It is the section of the story in which the forming hero realizes something is wrong with his or her world—that things could be so much better than they currently are—and sets out to do something about it.

This process of setting out is filled with all sorts of twists and turns, such that some who (in real life) think to start out immediately become discouraged and find that they have failed even to leave the confines of their living rooms. Have something on your mind you know you need to do but never do? Act one reveals why.

In act one we follow the hero (and by implementation your future journey) through the call to adventure, the refusal of the call, acquiring supernatural aid, crossing the first threshold, and entering the belly of the whale. These stages correspond to real psychological and interpersonal states of being, and the heroes of the monomyth reveal to us how we ought to respond to these states for the best possible outcome in life.

In story and myth, we find and love the hero. In our books, television shows, and movies, we encounter humans who clearly set themselves apart. Through cunning or supernatural power, they prove themselves able to face the failures of their worlds head-on and in the end prevail, creating worlds healthier and more beautiful. Heroes fight for justice, for freedom, for transformation. Heroic stories touch our hearts and fill us with inspiration. They speak to deep longings in the human soul. Far too often, however, our own lives are only facsimiles of what they could be. We long to become the hero we see in our favorite show or movie or novel but struggle with the immense difficulties and challenges that encompass real life. In the end, we give up, resign ourselves to normality, and embrace a boring job to pay our bills and stay alive. The life we long for is too difficult to attain, requires too much work.

Religion and self-help books offer some semblance of freedom, promising outlandish returns but focusing only on the most positive aspects of our souls. "You are amazing!" they cry to us, as if that declaration alone is enough to transform our inner and outer worlds.

It is not. Surprisingly, however, it is in the very stories and myths of religion that we find the keys to transformation. Those keys do not lie in the explicit teachings—"be kind to one another"—but within the story fabric in which they are told. It is in the story itself that we find inherent universal human truth. The spoken teachings point only at the result of what has happened within the being, the person who is at the focal point of the story.

That last statement may surprise the scholar of religion, who has learned that the miraculous life of the saint or religious founder exists solely to provide a platform for religious dogma. However, through a survey of ancient religion and culture, such as in Joseph Campbell's work *The Hero with a Thousand Faces*, we find that it is not the teachings that are universal but the miraculous story itself! It is the miraculous story of birth, life, death, and rebirth that we find constantly and consistently throughout culture, race, and religion.

It is in this miraculous story that all the power, psychological and supernatural, is held. And it is through this story that we may come to a better grasp of our present-day reality and struggle. This myth, or monomyth, repeated throughout every historical social group of the world is the real story, the meat of the matter wherein we find the keys for self-transformation and actualization.

With that in mind, I hope you will join me on an enlightening journey of self-discovery. Throughout the pages of this book, you will find applicable steps that will transform you into yourself, into your true nature that all the heroes of humanity desired you would find before the veil of time obscured the story's hidden meaning.

1

CALL TO ADVENTURE

The boy sat on a rock overlooking fields of green. In the valley below, his sheep grazed, warmed by the light of the sun. All of a sudden, a light shone about him. Looking around, he was surprised to find an old man standing only a few feet away, bent over and leaning heavily on his staff.

"Who are you?" the boy asked.

"Adventure," the man whispered.

Puzzled, the boy was about to ask what the old man meant, but just then the old crone burst into a million white dandelion puffs. The wind blew, and the puffs fluttered through the air, blinding the boy for a moment before floating into the sky.

Struck with wonder, the boy watched as they dispersed, until only the memory of them remained.

Starting the Journey

The call to adventure represents that innate calling we all hold and know: that life could be better than it is. This is the stage you are in when you start out. It is likely the stage you are in currently—although as you sit reading, you may indeed already have started out and be at one stage or another along the path. However, regardless of where you are, the thoughts and exercises in this chapter will be helpful to you along the way.

This is the stage of the journey where you have the opportunity to look around and say, "I don't like that about my life!" or, "I'm not satisfied with this!" It is also the stage in which a spark of wonder may come along and remind you that things could be so much better.

The universe is calling to you. If you have not already arrived in life, if your life could be so much better than it is, then all you need to do is ask, and listen.

Ask, how could I make my world a better place? What destiny exists inside me I have yet to achieve? What dreams have I given up on, that I used to long for?

Your dream is the first guide. It is the call. Your dream is the voice that tells you what could be—and as you start out, you must first hear this voice—this deep, inner voice that tells you of the destiny that could be.

Throughout this book, my goal is that you will not only learn about the stages of this journey and how they may manifest in your life but also go through exercises related to each stage so you will meet them successfully. The goal is to help you be successful along the journey so that you can see it through to completion.

In life we all start out on this journey at one point or another. Those who complete this journey, however, are as rare as the winners of Nobel Prizes and Academy Awards, as senators and congressmen, and as mega-corporate CEOs. They are the 0.01 percent. And formulaic though it may sound, this journey and the exercises related to it are key to taking you closer to their high abode. It is both an inner and outer journey—one which will draw you towards your outward potential, and take you deep within the walls of your inner abode. On this journey you will transform, you will grow, and yes, you will fulfill the dream of your heart—your destiny.

The First Kind of Call

The first kind of call to adventure starts out something like this. There you are, sitting in your boring job, fulfilling your boring duties, living your boring life. You are frustrated. You have not lived up to everything you thought you would.

Unbeknownst to you, however, the universe is constantly seeking one who will answer to its call. You don't know it, but at this very moment all the forces of the cosmos are searching for one like you—a hero! You may not think you are a hero, and you may not be one right now. But the universe sees your deep potential, and if you think about it, I think you can see it as well.

You know that there is something special inside of you, a deep spark of life that calls out to be great, to live a life of dreams fulfilled. And deep within, you feel the dream stirring, the vision rising. It was your call, your long-forgotten destiny. Maybe you tried, you set out to accomplish it, but found failure along the way and settled for less than the greatness you expected.

However, the universe is calling you still, today, at this very moment. It is calling you, in the quiet whispering of the dreams that could be and of the greatness you could accomplish in the world!

The first kind of call, then, is a personal call to change your life for the better. It is the call to accomplish your dreams, to fulfill your destiny. And no matter what anyone may tell you, there is nothing wrong in the least with this kind of call. In fact, if you find this kind of call present in your life, you will likely do the universe and everyone around you a great favor by completing it (not to mention yourself). Many great heroes have arisen in this way, and our world is much better for them.

The Second Kind of Call
Now, there is a second kind of person whom I want to address briefly: you are the kind who is very satisfied with your life. The hero's journey, if you mean to embark on it at all, may be the kind of journey that is not your own but another's. This kind of journey is very grand indeed. You do not need to be dissatisfied with life to set out to become a hero.

Remember Bilbo Baggins. He was very satisfied, was he not? In fact, he was so satisfied with his life that he "Good morninged" Gandalf four or five times! Bilbo had everything his heart desired—comfort; a nice, cozy home; and the respect of his neighbors and peers. Gandalf, however, saw something else in Bilbo. Gandalf saw a hidden greatness, a secret hero-ism even Bilbo didn't know or understand, and seeing this called Bilbo away on a grand adventure. And by the time the adventure was over, Bilbo was extremely thankful to Gandalf for interrupting his comfortable life. If I am speaking to you, then know that your adventure—the one in which you will be transformed into a true hero—will come to you from without, and often you will be called to it by another. Here, Bilbo's at-tempt to get Gandalf to leave is his refusal of the call, which will be the topic of the next chapter. However, what I wanted to draw your attention to was just how satisfied with ordinary life Bilbo was.

Gathering the Vision

This stage of the journey is the stage in which you must identify, at least in some form or fashion, what the *goal* of your quest is. Of course, the goal you start out with may not be the goal you finish with, or it may end up being a goal you complete but find to be only the beginning of a much grander and more miraculous ending. For example, Bilbo does not set out to find the ring—on the contrary, Gandalf and his dwarves claim only to seek the treasure of Smaug's lair. However, along the way, Bilbo does discover the ring, and as we know, that is the real treasure that leads to a much grander adventure later on for Frodo.

What is important is that you have a clearly defined goal in mind. What do you, by this adventure, hope to accomplish? Riches, wealth, fame? Those goals are not evil, in and of themselves, but they are very likely only a small piece of the puzzle. Furthermore, as we will find out in the chapter "Supernatural Aid," the degree to which your goal aligns with the goals of society as a whole will determine the amount of exterior aid you receive.

Therefore, if you are just starting out, it is worth taking the time to think through not only what your personal goal is but how you can accomplish it in a way that benefits the world around you. On the other hand, if you are going to have an adventure of the second type—the kind of being carried away by the group, much like Bilbo—then you needn't worry so much with defining the goal yourself, as it will be defined for you. Society, in this case, will be clearly crying out with some need or goal, and you will join yourself to the quest. Simply look around your life, and ask whether there is some injustice in the world you care about so deeply that you might actually be willing to do something about it.

Preparations for the Call to Adventure

When you are setting out on a new adventure, start by taking an inventory of your current life situation. What things come to mind that you do not like very much? Where are your frustrations? Where are you dissatisfied? These are great places to begin thinking about where and how you can grow. They will reveal to you areas of your life in which you are not complete. The areas of dissatisfaction or frustration reveal to you something that is missing in your life.

If you follow these inner urges, you will find a vision of how things could be better or an outcome you would like to achieve. Here you start to form the beginnings of your journey. The outcome you now have in mind will create the excitement and motivation necessary to change. You will say to yourself, "If I could only be…then I would…"

And once you have encapsulated your dream or vision, then the journey will begin.

Furthermore, at this stage you will either realize there is quite a lot you would like to change in your life or not very much at all. If you realize there is not much you would like to change, then you may realize your call will be the second type, the adventure that is not your own. Even as you read these words, some friend or relative, or even a people group or part of society, may come to mind.

This person or group who comes to mind—who may truly be struggling in life—is the beginning of your call. Helping them, fighting for them, assisting them in completing their mission in life, this will form the basis of your own grand quest. However, you need not worry about the adventure being a completely selfish one—you will gain your own share in the treasure, after all, just as Bilbo did when he joined Gandalf's dwarves. And in the end, remember, although Bilbo set out on an adventure that was not his own, he ended up finding a treasure that was much grander than the original goal.

So too it will be for you, if you set out on this second type of call. If this is the case, recognize it, and begin to think about how you can help heal the world and others. What person or group is in need that you could assist? Maybe a friend or acquaintance is just starting to do something great for herself, but she will need your assistance along the way. Should you join her on her journey? The answer belongs to you and you alone.

Finally, knowing whether it is your own call or another's, take the time to define your goal. Although it may change over the course of the journey, it is of vast importance to have the goal in mind now, while you are setting out, so you can know where you are going. Each of the stages will require something of you, in its own way, and you must be willing to allow your call to change.

However, it cannot change if it does not even exist. Therefore, no matter how selfish the call may seem today—or indeed how egalitarian—it still must be formed. As you think, try to define the specific outcome you would like to see by the end of the journey.

What do you hope to achieve? What do you hope to gain? What change would you like to see in your life? Answer these questions as you are setting out, and you will have plenty of motivation to continue as trial and challenge come your way (for they surely will).

2

REFUSAL OF THE CALL

Pondering the sudden appearance of the old crone and his miraculous act of vanishing, the boy sat some time more on that old rock. The day grew cold, however, and the boy, putting aside thoughts of the old man who called himself Adventure, set about gathering his flock for the night.

Later, having returned home for dinner, he told his father about the old man, but his father just laughed.

"Rubbish," he said. "Fairy tales aren't real."

That night, the boy lay awake, thinking of the man. His father, thought the boy, was right. He had just imagined the entire episode.

The First Refusal

Having heard the call of destiny clearly, you may be excited to begin your journey at once. Invariably, however, as you start out you will suddenly realize how very hard accomplishing your dream will be. When you do you will likely shrink back and wonder whether you ought to do it at all.

This is the first refusal. Having seen at once the real difficulty of the matter, it is simply the normal psychological reaction of the human being to withdraw. If the answers to the questions at the end of the previous chapter seemed far too grandiose for the nonchalant way in which the questions were asked—welcome, traveler, to the refusal of the call!

The refusal of the call is a state of life we may find ourselves in far too often—we know that things could be better, yet because of the difficulty of changing, we refuse to do anything about it. By examining this stage, you may gain the strength to move forward on your path. This discussion may feel heavy to you as you read it, but I encourage you to continue—here you will gain the wisdom to start out and move forward with your destiny. Understanding this place in your life will give you the strength to move past it, to defeat the doubts that hinder and to launch you forward into your life calling.

If you find yourself in situations you know are not the best yet do nothing to change them, you may have found yourself in the refusal-of-the-call stage. In story and myth, this stage is usually very brief. In real life, however, it may last months or years and be a period of stagnation in which we refuse to change. Many sink into this state semipermanently. Think of the addict who, knowing his addiction is causing him pain and that he ought to quit, says, "I will quit when I'm ready." However, what he is really saying is, "When my addiction has caused me more pain than I can bear, that is the day I will be ready to embrace the difficulty that comes along with changing."

Or maybe you have ventured out on the path once or many times, only to be beaten back by some giant along the way, some temptation too grand to resist—and having failed time and time again, beaten by your own personal demons, you may have given up on the call to adventure entirely, instead searching for any easier route through life. If this is you, then you have given up and settled for less than your destiny.

In that case, I am extremely excited that you are reading this book! In the following pages, my aim is to elucidate the path you must take to achieve success on your personal journey and mission in life. Additionally, I hope to equip you with the tools and strategies you will need to vanquish your demons, defeat the dragons, overcome the temptations, and achieve victory.

Is It the Right Quest?

If you are in this circumstance, there could be several causes. One is that you may be attempting some feat of grandeur beyond your current strength or skill. If that is the case, it does not mean you must give up on your dream—only that you must readjust your course, completing some "side quests" to "level up," so to speak. That is perfectly OK!

Furthermore, by reading this book and thinking through the questions at the end of each chapter, you will be able to clearly perceive and define whether you are ready for your chosen quest. You will also find that any goal worth attaining will come with temple guardians equal to its call, with temptations at least as strong as the true wealth at the completion of the journey. As in Isaac Newton's third law of motion, which states, "For every action, there is an equal and opposite reaction," any good you wish to bring into this world will be accompanied by forces of darkness of equal strength and tenacity, which you will need to displace before achieving your goal. It cannot be any other way.

Now you may see, if you have failed so many times that you have given up, it could simply be that the dragon guarding that specific destiny is simply a bit too strong for you as you currently are. In that case, simply redefining your desired outcome to a goal proportionate with your current level of strength or skill will allow you to achieve success.

Furthermore, with one or two successes under your belt, you will find that demons that once loomed large and insurmountable now seem manageable or even conquerable. The goal, in this regard, is not to set out to become a world hero overnight. Rather, it is to repeat the process of the hero's journey countless times, starting with perhaps a personal goal that is a challenge, but completable, and moving on to larger and larger victories in life so that over the years you can look back at a long string of growing victories and realize the journey has played out on a macro scale in addition to the micro scale you may have initially envisioned. In my concluding remarks (and perhaps another book altogether), I will touch on this idea of macro and micro scales in the hero's journey and investigate how they may play out in our lives.

Making All the Right Preparations
There is also the possibility that the trials defeated you not because they were too strong or powerful for you but because you had simply failed to prepare for them. Maybe the guidance you were given was incomplete and failed to mention that as you embarked on your quest, a giant demon or temptation would immediately appear out of the woodwork to swallow you up and prevent you from taking even one step along the path. If that is the case, one of the surest ways to victory is simply to understand the value of the goal you are setting out

to accomplish. (I will touch on this in detail in the chapter "Woman as Temptress.") Having the goal and its value to you clearly described will be the key that allows you to overcome temptation and prepare for the trials you will meet.

Completing this exercise will also clarify to you whether the goal you have chosen is even worth the trouble—you may have thought at first how nice it would be if such and such were to happen. However, having counted the cost, you may find that it really is not worth the trouble at all. Many times failure comes to us when we fail to count the cost and naively run after whatever treasure crosses our path. Before we set out on this journey, it is of the utmost importance that we ensure every step along the way aligns with our inner goals and drive.

Of course, it is not always possible to know in advance who you truly are, and in life, some failure is inevitable. You are on a journey of self-discovery—missteps along the way are to be expected. Let us only ensure that we learn from them, discover more fully who we are, and not make the same mistakes again in the future.

Right of First Refusal
You may be just starting out. This may be your first time along the hero's journey, and you may have initially (when you saw this book and picked it up, for example) thought how grand that would be to become your own personal hero. As you turn the pages of this book and find the trials and temptations that wait, you may grow afraid and decide that the hero's journey is not, after all, for you. This is, essentially, the classical idea of refusal of the call, and if you find yourself in such a state, the universe may decide to send you some help to dislodge you from your complacency.

However, if we choose to run from our call (when the real call of our life appears), then we should know upfront that we may well be running the rest of our natural lives. Take, for example, Joseph Campbell's illustration of King Minos:

> "His flowering world becomes a wasteland of dry stones and his life feels meaningless—even though, like King Minos, he may through titanic effort succeed in building an empire of renown. Whatever house he builds, it will be a house of death: a labyrinth of cyclopean walls to hide from him his Minotaur. All he can do is create new problems for himself and await the gradual approach of his disintegration."

In the end, of course—unlike in books or movies—no one can control your fate or destiny. If you truly wish to refuse the call and fight to the bitter end for mediocrity, then no one can stop you. This book is merely a guide map for the quest, attempting to elucidate the path and make its journeying that much easier.

It is also important to note that we can trick ourselves in answering our call to adventure. Maybe we have set the goal for ourselves—"I want to be rich"—when the exterior reality and forces of the cosmos are crying out for us to find some higher calling, some adventure wherein we will lose ourselves and become joined to some vastly higher power. If this is true, only time will tell, but it may behoove us to think about whether we have truly set a goal for ourselves that is in alignment with our highest nature.

Joseph Campbell also draws from the Bible in this regard:

"Because I have called, and ye refused...I also will laugh at your calamity; I will mock when your fear cometh; when your fear cometh as desolation, and your destruction cometh as a whirlwind; when distress and anguish cometh upon you."

In the exercises below, take some time to think through whether there is any call you have refused. Doing so does not necessarily mean you must embark on that refused adventure today—but it may give you the clarity, throughout the rest of these exercises, to understand more fully just what destiny you are running from and why you are running from it. Then, psychologically speaking, you may be ready to embark again anew.

Preparations for Refusal of the Call
The refusal of the call usually comes early in the journey. When you arrive at this stage, doubts and trepidation will start to fly. The voices of worry and doubt will raise their ugly heads. You must meet them head-on. Ask yourself what scares you most about your chosen call. OK, now how can you overcome that voice of fear? In what way will you defeat that apparent roadblock?

What could go wrong on your journey? Brainstorming the possible roadblocks and setbacks at the outset is not a bad thing—it is a natural part of life. It is here, in these brainstorming sessions, that we find we are enough. Answering the voices of doubt affirmatively gives us psychological confidence to move forward. Knowing that we have triumphed once or twice or several times already within the confines of our mind gives us the confidence to move forward in the physical world with our call.

Maybe you have set out in the past to do something great and failed. If so, the memories of those failures will likely come back to haunt you. Do not run from them, but defeat them. Answer them now wisely. Define stratagems by which you will overcome every previous failure. How will this time be different? Put it into writing if necessary. You will overcome by such and such a method, and this is why you will not fail this time. This is how you can be sure you will proceed victoriously.

On the other hand, maybe in the past you attempted to do something truly great but failed because you were not yet ready in your development. Ask yourself how can you change your goal, modify it by making it more attainable as you are today. By doing so, you can experience success through making your goal smaller and gain confidence, momentum, skill, and wisdom to take on true giants later on, after you have finished one or two smaller adventures in life.

Do not allow doubt to defeat you, and neither run from it. Meet it head-on, and answer it wisely—overcome it, and prove to yourself that you really will accomplish your journey. On the other hand, if the doubt does overwhelm you, that is OK. That simply means the goal you have thought up is not really your goal. Maybe you do not possess the skill to take that specific giant on—it was a good idea but maybe for someone else.

In that case, do not move blindly forward knowing unanswered doubts linger that you find unable to defeat. You must possess wisdom to do anything great. You must know, at the outset, whether you truly are the one called to this specific adventure. You have a calling, and it is grand. You must simply find the calling that is correct for you in your specific stage of maturity.

3

SUPERNATURAL AID

The next day the boy set out with his flock across the fields and, coming to a stream, thought to let them water a bit. Pausing, he sat down on a nearby rock, but no sooner did he recline than once again a flash of blinding light drew his attention.

The boy turned, and there once more was the old man, leaning on his weathered and knotted staff.

"You again!" the boy exclaimed.

"Well, are you ready for your adventure?" the old man asked.

"But, you're not real!"

"So says your father," the man responded. "What do you say?"

"I suppose…you look real enough," the boy said. "But what do you mean, Adventure?"

"Over the hills and through the mountain pass, there lies a temple in which they teach the ancient ways. It is said in this very generation lives a boy who will grow to be the next ascended master. Maybe you will be that boy."

"M-me?" the boy said. "I could never be a great master."

"Oh?"

The boy looked back toward the valley that hid the house of his father. In the distance, a dark cloud overshadowed the horizon, and below men on horses rode across the valley ridge.

"The time grows short," the old man said. "Will you go or not?"

"O-OK!" the boy blurted out.

With that, the old man lurched forward with a speed that surprised the boy and forced into his hands a small golden amulet.

"Take this!" the man said. "You will need it! Now go! Remember, through the mountain pass is the way to the temple!"

And with that the old man burst once more into a million dandelion puffs, lost at once to the wind.

The World's Gift

Congratulations! By making this far, you have overcome the first roadblock to your success! With doubt destroyed, the universe will now reward you with a sudden and instantaneous boost. That boost is known as supernatural aid.

Stepping out on the road of adventure can be a scary experience, but you can embrace the process and dive in headlong, knowing that almost as soon as you begin to move in the direction of your dream, the universe will respond by sending you the help you need to get started.

This is known as the stage of supernatural aid. (Some call it beginner's luck, but that would be to miss the point entirely.)

This stage represents the help the exterior world grants when we are ready or at the critical moment along the path. The universe provides this aid because the following stages into which we will step will prove to be beyond our abilities to deal with as we presently are.

The stage of supernatural aid comes just after the journey has begun. You could even go so far as to call it the real start of the journey, but let's not discount setting out itself. In the previous two stages, we discussed the motivation to change, what is called the call to adventure, and the psychological processes we naturally go through as we shift into embracing that call, what is known as the refusal of the call. Remember, it was in the second stage that we refuse to embrace the call because we realize it entails trials or difficulties that may be too much for us.

When you have come to terms with your adventure, when you have your goal firmly in mind, and when you have made the necessary psychological preparation to embark on it, then what is known as supernatural aid will appear.

From *The Hero with a Thousand Faces*:

> One has only to know and trust, and the ageless guardians will appear. Having responded to his own call, and continuing to follow courageously as the consequences unfold, the hero finds all the forces of the unconscious at his side. Mother Nature herself supports the mighty task. And in so far as the hero's act coincides with that for which his society itself is ready, he seems to ride on the great rhythm of the historical process.

Having overcome the barriers of doubt and decided earnestly to progress, the universe will reward your daring with supernatural energy to propel you forward—outside help, like a kind friend reaching down to pull you up, or a wise counselor to show you how to proceed. With the aid granted, it is time to embrace the momentum—walk through the open doors and begin to accelerate towards your destiny.

It is also important to keep a watchful eye out at this point. If supernatural aid does not appear, you may ask yourself whether your "act coincides with that for which…society itself is ready," because to the extent to which it does, you will "seem to ride on the great rhythm of the historical process," as we have read in the work of Joseph Campbell. This is the supernatural aid we speak of. It is Mother Nature manifesting itself supernaturally on your behalf to aid you in the journey for which you set out, which is also aligned to a great degree with the need of your surrounding society.

Of course, you may wonder at this point whether the universe aid you in accomplishing your personal dream. Of course it will! Fulfilling your destiny will be of untold benefit to the world and society around you. Any great work you create will heal and aid the world, and so the world will assist you in beginning your quest. The kind of journey which the universe will not aid is the kind where you are setting out to do something entirely selfish, or something which is not really your destiny. If you are running from your real call, for example, you will find a definite lack of supernatural aid to help you along.

If you find yourself lacking in supernatural aid, you may ask whether the journey you have chosen is truly the dream of your heart, your real destiny, or if it is some form of running from your destiny. If you are running from your real call, you may be forced to brave the trials alone. In that case, I suggest—especially if you are just starting out—that you revisit the call to adventure and ensure your quest is for the benefit of the world, of society, and is also the fulfillment of your heart's deepest desires. To the degree with which you align your quest with the needs and aspirations of the greater society and world, you will you receive supernatural aid along the journey. Generally, even if the call is of the first kind, it will do some good for this world we all call home.

The Aid Already Given

I would also say here that if you have started and stopped several times over (in the case of having tried and failed more times than you can count, for example), you may indeed be overladen with supernatural aid already. In that case, I would not concern yourself too much with whether supernatural aid at once appears. The universe may be tired of giving you aid if you have not properly used what it has already given you.

If you believe that could be true, for this stage, simply spend a while thinking over the times you started previously and the aid that was given to you—it may be a word of wisdom or some assistance you received. It is very likely that, not knowing the path, you did not recognize the aid for what it was when it came. Every day the universe is watching out for us, trying to help us here and there along our path.

Once you have remembered the aid already given, meditate on those gifts, and ask how you can implement them now, today, as you start again. You will likely need them, and dull as they may be, they will no doubt still hold that supernatural power that will help you overcome the obstacles in your path.

Preparations for Supernatural Aid

One of two things—and perhaps both, as you really get started—will now begin to happen.

First, you will find that in your life, supernatural aid has been abundantly provided whenever you have really needed it. Think back to anytime you have tried to do something in your life. Has there not been some provision, some gift such as a mentor or guide, some wise counselor who spontaneously appeared to help you?

Not knowing that this was indeed such an element in life, you likely carried on your way, thanking the person for his or her advice but never really realizing the divine element in the conversation you just had.

These conversations have purpose. When we have made up our mind to do something, they help us start by getting us ready to succeed where we alone would surely fail. The quest, indeed, is currently far beyond our power to complete alone. We have never been there before, never followed that road to its conclusion. But those who have come before us have— they know the way, know what you must do in order to be successful.

And though they love you, in your youth and naivety they see how many things could easily go wrong. They will realize how unprepared you are, but having once started out themselves, they remember a time when they, too, were young and unready for the trials of life. However, through their youth and tenacity, they surely triumphed, and they long for you to do so as well.

It is the grace of the mentors and the joy of the counselors to see a younger generation rise up without quite as much difficulty as they themselves had in getting where they are today.

The counselors' or guides' quests long ago completed, they now find their joy in helping you.

The second way the Supernatural Aid stage will appear will be altogether new aid. As you start to venture forth the universe will begin to respond to your movement. Once you have moved forward, used up the aid of the past, and recollected what came before, now the universe, noticing your momentum and ability and just how much you have grown, will bend itself to help you.

Better and stronger aid than ever before will come—perfectly suited to your developmental level and ability to proceed. The aid will match your quest and help you proceed. For some starting out, Joseph Campbell refers to the hitchhiker miraculously picked up by just the right traveler to assist on the adventure.

Start first by thinking about the aid you have received in the past. Do everything you can to honor it. If it is still relevant, for example, try to put that wisdom into practice. Next, as you start out, prepare yourself by keeping a lookout for wise mentors who have gone the way you are going in the past. You will know them because they will have the marks of completion specific to your quest.

If the universe provides mentors who do not match your quest—for example, you hope to achieve some masterpiece of art, but the mentors around you are all religious leaders—know that they will not truly be of great assistance. Although they try to help where they can, when you are starting out, you need a guide who has been there before.

There is a guide for every quest—a mentor for every way. Make sure you follow the guide who is correct for the specific quest or journey you are going on. If the mentor does not yet

appear, do not worry—he or she will come when the time is right. Prepare yourself by knowing that when the time comes to start out, the universe will invariably give you some help along the way.

4

CROSSING OF THE FIRST THRESHOLD

The old man gone, the boy glanced once more to the valley of his home. The men on horses were now descending through the valley and seemed to be going from house to house. The boy couldn't be sure what they were doing, but he knew it wasn't good.

His heart was torn. He did not want to abandon his father and brothers, but what could he do against these dark men with swords? He was only a young shepherd boy. But perhaps, he thought, if he became the ascended master, he could return and save his family from the coming scourge.

Courage welling up within, he turned and rushed across the stream, passing through the forest toward the foothills and then at last to the foot of the mountain, where the rocks parted to the narrow mountain pass.

As he approached, however, in the opening he saw a horse and, atop the horse, a rider wrapped in a dark robe. Clutching the old man's amulet in his hands, the boy approached.

"Where are you going?" the man's voice thundered.

Closer now, the boy could see the man's face was hidden by a mask, and tied around his arm was a black band with a dark-red circle painted against it.

"To the temple that lies within the mountains," the boy replied.

"The way is closed. Return to your home to join the counting!" the man said.

At the boy's side, the amulet seemed to pulse, and from somewhere the boy was filled with sudden courage.

"I am going to the temple," he said once more.

However, the boy could no more than finish his sentence before the horse on which the man rode neighed, and the rider lifted a gleaming spear into the darkened sky. The next moment the horse was charging forward, the gleaming spear tip pointed directly at the boy's heart.

Scrambling, the boy dove to the side, and as he did, he raised his hands in defense against the oncoming spear.

A clash resounded, and a sudden burst of brilliant light blinded the boy. He opened his eyes a moment later to see the horse on its side some feet away, the dark rider thrown and lying on the ground, dead. The amulet, which he now remembered was clutched in his hands, had smashed against the spear and exploded from within.

Lifting himself from the ground, the boy approached the rider, stooped down, and removed the man's mask. The blood drained from the boy's face, however, as he looked, aghast, at the face of his brother.

Stumbling backward, he clutched the amulet—now broken by the tip of his brother's spear—and sped toward the mountain pass.

Beginning in Earnest

Hold on! You may be crying, "I don't want to kill my brother!" Don't worry; you won't have to—at least not literally. Remember, we are dealing with symbolic imagery here. Our goal in this book is to translate the images of myth into practically applicable tools for the modern life. So give me a moment, and I will explain the meaning.

The crossing of the first threshold is that moment of taking the plunge. It is a moment of transformation, an awakening, in which our eyes become open to a facet of reality we had not previously perceived. Often it has to do more with awakening to our inner world than our outer. It comes after we have already started out, after the universe has given us some supernatural aid, and is the first real trial along the way to our destiny.

It is also, however, wrought with difficulty. It is a moment of great challenge and is often a representation of embracing the dark unknown. Here we have truly begun our quest in earnest, and we must defeat the first guardian along the way. Although terrifying, anyone with skill and prudence can defeat these threshold guardians and cause the danger to fade away. This test is the first of many in which you, the new hero, must prove your readiness for the quest beyond.

If you have sufficiently prepared, you should be ready to dismiss these first challengers with ease. Psychologically, they may present themselves as the voices of discouragement, stating how difficult the challenge will be or warning of the insurmountable odds we will be forced to encounter along the way.

The Threshold Within

Now we find the great value of *knowing the path*. When we are mentally prepared for the voices of discouragement, darkness, and despair to come to us, then we can appreciate them as the factors by which we may judge our readiness to accomplish the task we have set out for ourselves.

If, for example, these voices of discouragement truly discourage us, it may be the case that we are not fully committed to the work we have chosen. Maybe our goal or quest is something we think would be nice to accomplish, but when push comes to shove, we realize the work isn't worth the effort. In order to pass this phase of the journey, commitment is key. We must be willing to defend our choice to progress along the path, make the sacrifices that arise, and continue.

If the threshold guardians succeed in turning us away, we may know that we have set out on the wrong quest for our current self. Either the quest is not our destiny altogether, or it is some destiny that is too far advanced, too difficult and out of reach.

This kind of preemptive planning allows us to ensure we are fully committed to the quest we have chosen. If you are reading this chapter now, take great care that you ensure your quest is worth the trouble. If it is, you will find answers to those voices of discouragement that arise. Otherwise, you will be totally discouraged, and I suggest you revisit your original goal, modify it, and then return to the threshold once more, ready to challenge the guardians and see if they let you pass.

From this vantage point, we realize the guardians are simply that: guards who prevent the unready hero from taking on more than he or she can bare and, having begun the quest in earnest, meet a terrible demise for which he or she was not well prepared.

If, on the other hand, as you set out along your journey, you find the voices of discouragement and fear not altogether terrifying, then you will find that they open to your path. They draw back and seem small and easily defeated. In that case, you should take it as a signal you are ready to advance. The threshold guardian, of course, is the least of the enemies you must vanquish along the way, but he serves as a baseline to know whether you at least possess enough wit and courage and drive to succeed. From here on out, the quest becomes ever more difficult and fraught with danger, and you must prove yourself worthy.

The Guardian Without
After having vanquished the personal, inner psychological voices of defeat and despair, be prepared as well for them to manifest in your reality. Having proven your mettle inwardly, it is likely the true guardian will sooner or later raise his head to test you in the outward world. For example, if you begin telling people, "I am going to do such and such," they may begin firing back at you with all the reasons why you can't do such a thing.

Luckily, however, you have already prepared for their concerns. In myth and in fairy tales, these guardians are depicted as a black knight or a dragon. The black knight, however, once he is defeated and his visor raised, turns out to be the hero's brother. This is how the "brother battle" comes to commonly symbolize the guardian of the first threshold. Often in life, those who will first attempt to prevent us from journeying out on our path of adventure will be those closest to us—our brother or sister or friend who seeks to prevent us from leaping into ruin foolishly and will therefore begin spouting out all the reasons why we *can't* do whatever it is we want to do. "Well, it will be too hard," they say. They do this out of love for us because they don't want us to begin something we cannot complete.

Preparation now, both inwardly and outwardly, using wisdom to listen to the voices of reason and complaint, will prepare us to meet that harsh reality ahead when it comes. And in our preparation, we may yet prove ourselves successful in the journey.

When the guardian does appear—whether in the friend or sibling you casually exclaim your profound dream or idea too—do not shrink back. Don't run in fear or denial. That is a sure way to your impending demise. Defeating this guardian—in real life, through argument and reason—will prove to yourself and the world that you are truly ready for the trial. Additionally, the guardian will present to you often some impending difficulty you had not yet thought of.

Although it may seem and feel at first as if this person wishes you not to succeed, he or she ultimately does you a favor. The guardian forces you to look at the problem from a different point of view and discover whether you have the answer to the challenges that reality will ultimately bring to you as you seek to complete your quest.

As a final note, in some stories the unmasked dark knight wears the face of the hero himself. You will know you have passed the test of the brother battle when, having responded to your friend's or sibling's concerns successfully, you later see in him or her your own failings or weakness. When you realize that person, too, is human and fallible, his or her previous concerns or complaints will vanish and fade, and you can be sure you have passed this stage of the quest.

Preparation for the First Threshold

Now the ebb and flow of story becomes applicable to daily life. Here we find the second of our resistances along the way. Where the refusal of the call highlighted doubt, crossing the first threshold highlights external discouragement and defeat. They are similar but not the same. Where the refusal of the call could be seen in the father telling his son not to go, the crossing of the first threshold is seen in the brother violently opposing his sibling's progress.

Internally, this can express itself psychologically as the voice of discouragement. "You will never succeed," this voice says. "It is too hard. Stop now."

Externally, it may be your closest friend or adviser telling you that you are not good enough, you will not be enough, and you should just stay put and not really do anything special. "You don't need to do it. Just be happy with what you have," they will say, and then they will list to you all the reasons why you *cannot.*

Do not shy away from this battle. Just as how in the refusal of the call the doubt had purpose, now, too, this violent opposition has purpose for your development. You must meet it head-on. In the internal world of your preparation, you have seen this battle coming. You are ready for it.

The brother battle will bring some voice of reason that you may not have thought of yet; there may be some hidden battle to come that you are not prepared for. Now is the time, instead of balking at the voice of discouragement, to embrace and overcome it. Meet it head-on with all the reasons why you *can*. This battle proves to both yourself and your closest external reality that you are ready for the challenges that lie ahead.

As your friend or sibling lists these reasons, keep your guard up and your wits about you. Do not allow their piercing blows to get under your armor or defeat you. Instead, respond to their complaints with a fierce tenacity of how you *will*. Remember, you are simply being made aware of the very real challenges ahead.

As you read this book, you may be tempted to go out at once and tell your closest friend or sibling or adviser what you plan to do, just to get the brother battle out of the way. I advise against this. First, complete the rest of this book. Along the way, your goal will morph and shape, you will learn and grow, and it may be that the goal you have in mind at the end of the reading will be vastly different from the one you are starting out with now.

This book is a map, and as a map, it will describe to you many more places you will go along your journey. Before setting out, you should know all the stops along the way. You may find that by the time you finish this book, your entire destination has changed, and in that case, you will be very glad to have held off on announcing your intentions to go before you really understood where you were going.

5

BELLY OF THE WHALE

The clouds crowded in overhead, casting deep shadows on the ravine. The boy's view of the clouds, however, was limited by the encroaching rock of the mountain pass above, and so he pressed on.

The way was steep and gradually tightened as he went so that his progress was slow, and he sometimes had to turn to one side or the other to progress. As he pushed forward, the rocks soon grew so tight that he cut himself on their edges, but the memory of his brother's dead face and the thought of his father pushed him on.

He had to make it to the mountain temple. It was his only choice now.

Soon the clouds broke, sending down a cold rain against the boy's skin. The sky became pitch-black, and the ravine wove back and forth through the mountains.

For a long while, the boy pushed forward. The broken amulet now clutched by his side was the only source of strength to keep him moving.

In the darkness, he stumbled and fell, scraping his knees and hands and hitting his head against the rock. Warm blood mixed with the cold, harsh rain, and in the darkness only the salt of his tears distinguished them from the rain.

Still he pushed on, ever clutching the broken amulet, until at last he stumbled out onto open ground and—the mountain walls no longer supporting his weight—collapsed.

In the distance, however, a bridge extended across a chasm, and there on the other side, a golden temple rose, its buttresses unoffended by the storm.

The Inner Temple

If the quest is one of intense inner transformation—such that your entire worldview is shattered in a single instant—then you may find yourself in the stage called belly of the whale. This stage, which may not always take place, represents that moment in which your soul, having perceived some altogether world-changing reality, now plunges into darkness and despair. This stage is momentary, however, and a grieving stage for that which we have known or perhaps for how wrong we have been about ourselves or the world around us.

Joseph Campbell describes it in this way: "The disappearance corresponds to the passing of a worshiper into a temple, where he is to be quickened by the recollection of who and what he is, namely dust and ashes unless immortal."

It is important to recognize as we discuss this stage that Joseph Campbell denotes it does not always take place. That is to say, it is not necessary for the hero's development on all types of heroic journeys.

Particularly, the kind of journey on which this stage will develop is one that requires an immediate transformation in the psychology of the hero—an instantaneous change that throws the hero into a temporary darkness, akin to a type of psychological crisis.

Perhaps as a teenager, having grown up in an entirely non-spiritual household, you suddenly have a spiritual awakening and realize how wrong your parents are to live the way they do in the world. Or, as a middle-age parent, you awake one day to find yourself absolutely miserable with your normal life and are thrown into a midlife crisis. These are belly of the whale–type experiences.

Inner Death and Awakening

This crisis is represented in myth and metaphor by the hero entering the belly of the whale, into a place of symbolic death and darkness from which he again emerges, perhaps cutting the whale open or maybe being deposited on dry land, such as in the story of Jonah. It is not usually described as a full death, such as in the crucifixion, but rather a death of the self and ego that prepares the hero for the journey ahead.

When it takes place, it is the last stage of the journey in the ordinary world. Furthermore, it marks the distinct transition into the inner or special world. It is in this inner world the hero will undergo his or her metamorphosis. In life, it will typically happen to an individual only once or not at all, although exceptions do occur.

Generally, this stage will take place if our journey is one of self-realization or enlightenment, when the scales suddenly fall from our eyes and we realize the entire life we have been living is nothing more than a dream or lie. Suddenly we find

HERO

ourselves in rebellion, like a teenager who has just grown up a little and has the realization that her parents are fools to be working and living as they are when there is a huge world full of spiritual wonder just beyond their fingertips.

The darkness of the whale signifies our sudden realization of the darkness in which we have been living all along. Sometimes, as in Jonah, this darkness comes to us because of our refusal of the call. Other times it is simply highlighted by the suddenly bright state of our inner world, enlightened by our awakening, before the inner light has had a chance to spread outward to our surroundings.

At this point, we also realize that we do not have the power to transform our outer world, yet. The darkness stands in great contrast to the light within. It guides us forcefully to the transformation we must make and the journey we must go on to change our world. The contrast serves to heighten our resolve now that we have embarked on the quest. It marks a point of no return—once your eyes are open to the darkness and the light within has begun to shine, there can be no turning back. Instead, embrace the adventure in front of you, for it will transform you into a force for good that will change your world to outwardly resemble the new light that shines within.

Preparations for the Belly of the Whale
If you do find yourself in this stage, the worst thing you can do is try at once to change everyone around you. Although you may suddenly see in your family everything wrong with the world, it is a mistake to attempt to fix it at this stage. In reality, you see reflected in them all your own personal failings. What you must do now is take a moment to grieve this passage and

let go of your attachment to how things are. You are just starting out on this journey.

Do not allow the darkness around you to hold you back.
Of course, this is not really an internal state of opposition
but closer to a stage of forward momentum expressing itself
darkly. You will in all likelihood be so fed up with life as it was
that there can be no going back. You will find yourself in tears
or disgusted with the world, and the momentum gained from
crossing the first threshold will send you hurtling forward.
Though the time is dark, it need not last long.

Resolve within yourself to change. Having this resolve,
step forward into the journey of life. When you conclude this
journey, you will be able to return to your family and friends
victorious, healed and transformed inwardly, and offer outwardly true change and transformation.

Since this stage takes place in only some journeys—and
because it is the topic of extensive religious literature—I will
not spend too much time on it. Furthermore, if you suddenly
find yourself in the blackest pit of despair at realizing your
entire world has turned upside down and is not what you once
thought it was, you will need more than anything the contents
of the next chapter. With that in mind, let us not stay here
long but move forward expediently on the journey.

Only know this one thing: you do not need to remain here
long, and the way out is simply to fully embrace your new call
in life.

Step forward.

ACT TWO

The Inner World

If you have made it this far, congratulations! You are now (or will be when you have started) well on your way to personal mastery and transformation. Act two details the meat of the journey. It is often the longest section of a story and generally where we will spend the most of our time.

In act two, you may find that what you thought was going to be a simple journey of fixing something in your life suddenly becomes an incredibly deep, life altering gateway to self-discovery. Embrace the profundity. Whether your goal is small and personal or world changing in scope, the process will transform you. You will grow; you will change. At the journey's end, you will be a hero of the real world. And whether the mastery you have gained is personal or societal, you will have glimpsed a realization of your true nature.

The transformation sparked by the journey will prepare you to accomplish countless other incredible feats in life. The journey doesn't end with the conclusion of one goal. On the contrary, you will be astounded to see how much you have grown when the final curtain falls, and that growth will spur you onward to even greater dreams.

There is an old saying, "Enjoy the journey," or, "Life isn't about the destination but the journey we take to get there." This saying has always felt a bit shallow to me—not knowing where I am going in life, how can I possibly enjoy the journey I am on? When it feels more like bouncing from place to place in life, overcome more by confusion than a systematic synthesis, what is there to enjoy?

Throughout the pages of this book, you will come to understand both your destination (act three) and the stages of life you will travel down to get there. With the understanding of where you are going and the steps you must take to get there, I hope "enjoying the journey of life" will become a much more realistic bit of advice. Now, knowing precisely where you are and what will come next, life may look more like a leisurely safari, or if that is too tame for a life that refuses to be tamed at any cost, then at least a theme-park ride like those we might find in Disneyland, where we are carted from one exciting surprise to the next but know we are really safe in the cart and will at last emerge into the light of day once more. We can experience the thrill of adrenaline for what it is, not actually fearing for our lives.

This section, then, regards the various stages of transformation that will take place after you have embraced the path and transitioned into the journey. These stages may require much—however, they will also grant the ultimate rewards in life. Completing them equates to attaining life success in the truest sense—not only material but emotional and spiritual wholeness that allow complete transformation of our life and world.

In this second section of your heroic journey, you will find the stages along the path dive more and more deeply into the realms of the subconscious. They become, as well, more and more spiritual in nature, such that the very soul of the intrepid hero, once an initiate, is transformed entirely. By the end of this section of the journey, the initiate becomes the hero-master of the world and returns with the power both to vanquish whatever foes lie in his way and right the wrongs committed by society in times past.

This second section is by far the most important section of the journey. In comparison, the significance of the first and third sections pale. Spiritually, this is the section of change, of inward transformation that prepares the hero to accomplish his task.

This section is also the most difficult to describe. In writing the following chapters, I found it surprisingly difficult to communicate several of the truths contained within. Along with their significance, they are the least willing to be bound and bent to reason. It is not a simple matter to describe these stages to the journeyman, nor do I hope thereby that you would accomplish their great mysteries at once.

Instead, several of the stages are themselves the primary focuses and central elements of various religions of the world. Tome after tome has been devoted to their study and explication, hoping the initiate may find some eternal truth and be transformed into the hero form set by the religious figure in question.

Indeed, most every world religion has at its center a great figure, an enlightened being or god-human who exemplifies the whole. He or she provides the perfect image of what the follower ought to become. And through his or her teaching, the religious devotee is to be perfected and transformed. Unfortunately, with such drastic and often necessary emphasis on the deep inner transformations, one tends to walk away from the great religions of the world with very little in the way of outward tools and usefulness to society.

As we will see in the opening of the next section of this journey, the temptation to remain in a state of eternal bliss does exist as a path one could take—never passing these inward mystical states to return to the world.

If one does turn to the religions of the world to gain entrance into these mystical states, she would be wise to take whatever teachings are given with a grain of salt. Remember, it is not the teachings themselves that appear to be universal truths of mankind—instead, it is the actual story-life of the teacher, the founder of whichever religion, that is the central and unchanging truth. Therefore, in this book we seek not to indoctrinate but to extract universal truth from all myth and mythos of the world, finding in the similar pattern universal truth that is applicable to the human conscious for its transformation and the benefit of the world.

Our goal, then, is not to become a devotee of any particular religion but to undertake our own hero journey of transformation and to stand shoulder to shoulder with those great teachers and leaders of the world, transformed by our understanding of universal truth and formed into the hero who saves the world.

In this section, I will first expound on the various states of mystical union and their specific abilities to transform our mind and conscious. I will not claim to be able herein to actually bring you through those states or introduce you to them directly—that is a journey you must endeavor to take yourself. I will, however, hope to provide a grid of understanding, a crash course, if you will, in the various mystical states of union commonly found throughout the stories of humanity. I will ground you in a very little taste of what those stories generally look like, address the psychological aspect of those states, communicate briefly the spiritual ramifications of such states, and then attempt to prepare you for those states with some brief thought exercises.

Particularly, four stages that can be described as various types of mystical union will be discussed. Mystical union is of central importance to the world hero, who cannot truly accomplish any task of great significance without it. The four stages—meeting with the goddess, atonement with the father, apotheosis, and ultimate boon—all describe different ways this mystical union can take place.

Very rarely does any one story feature all four. However, all four are necessary to one degree or another for full understanding of the human experience. Depending on your personal quest, you may rely more on one or two than the others. In common storytelling, we often see a mixture of at least two, sometimes three, but rarely all four.

The other two stages of this section are essential to nearly every hero of every kind. They are the road of trials and the woman as temptress. Both will be indispensable to the budding hero as he or she journeys to achievement.

This book is one of preparation. From the beginning, my hope was to prepare you for the heroic journey—to help you understand what forms and shapes that journey commonly takes. Like a road map, clearly revealed, I hope to make it far easier for you to start and complete the journey. However, like a map, which stays ever on a piece of paper (or in today's world, on the screen of your smart phone), this book will not be the journey itself. Only you can take that journey. I hope, however, that if you know the way, you will find it far easier to enter into this journey in your daily life and, facing myriad challenges along the way, know exactly which course to take to arrive swiftly at your desired destination.

May it be a wonderful journey of enlightenment and transformation.

6

THE ROAD OF TRIALS

Half-unconscious, the boy hardly noticed as he was lifted from the rocky ground and carried the rest of the way across the bridge. The rain had weakened to a soft patter now, and looking up into the face of his rescuer, he saw the eyes of the most beautiful girl he had ever glimpsed in his life.

Later, within the confines of the mountain temple, dried with a towel wrapped about him, an old monk sat facing the boy, his wizened eyes skeptical at best.

"Any initiate who wishes to become the ascended master must pass three tests before he can begin his trial in earnest," he said. "But be warned, all who have come before you have failed even to gain entrance to the inner sanctum. Are you sure you will be the one to succeed?"

Thinking of his father and his valley, the boy raised his chin toward the ancient monk.

"I am," he said.

M . A . S T E P H E N S O N

"Fine. Then your training begins at once. Follow me."

The monk led the boy to a sparring room, where he gave him a wooden sword and commenced to teach him the art of swordplay. Day after day the monk and the boy battled, until at last the boy bested the monk and held the point of his wooden sword to the monk's face.

"Very good," the monk said. "Now for your second test."

Now the boy was led to a room full of thin wooden posts and forced to jump from one to another, countless times falling into the pit of sand below. At last, he made it to the end where the monk awaited him.

"Good. Now, one last test," he said.

It was in the last room that the monk taught the boy the art of breathing and how to commune with nature.

"This," the monk said, "is the gift you will need the most when that day comes. When you are able to call a raven to this room without moving from the spot on which you sit, you will be ready to proceed."

So the boy sat. The sun rose, and the sun set. The moon rose, and the moon set. Over and over again, the cycle repeated itself, the boy unmoving until at last, dawn just on the horizon, a small black raven fluttered through the skylight and, as if to prove its point, landed directly in the boy's lap.

"Very well," the monk said with a laugh. "You may proceed. Tomorrow your true test will commence. Until then, you may rest."

Enter the Dragon

S etbacks. Resistance. Unexpected difficulty.

As you move forward on your path to realizing your dream, the universe will invariably throw countless trials, large and small, in your way. The good you seek to create will not be allowed to enter the world untried. These little setbacks serve to test your mettle. Here you must prove yourself to the world.

Focus one hundred percent on your goal. Where the test is one of skill, master your craft. Where it is one of adversity, overcome it with internal strength. The trials make you strong—they prepare you for the real battles to come.

At this point in the journey, you will have perceived reality in a new and drastically different way. You have begun to adjust to the ramifications of your new perspective, but just as you do, you will be confronted with the sudden need to learn a new set of skills and abilities that will allow you to live comfortably in your new world. There are great battles ahead, and the purpose of this journey is not to live in and enjoy the new world but to master it and ensure that when you return to the real, you do so with every weapon at your disposal to achieve complete victory.

In reality, you must understand and be prepared for the resistance that will come with any change you seek to implement in the world. This preparation is critical to your success. Not being prepared is the most frequent cause of failure to becoming the hero you seek to be. This stage consists of real applied preparation for the final battle that awaits you at the conclusion of the journey.

It must be said here that life often throws our way unexpected challenges and difficulties. This happens with such a degree of regularity, especially when we attempt to produce or do anything of true greatness, that it comes to be expected.

The point of this chapter, however, is not only to discuss the challenges that will come but to give you guidance on how to anticipate those trials in advance—by knowing that the trials prepare us bit by bit for our grand finale, our final battle moment, we can gain some expectation that they will come and soften the blow when they do. We do this by sharpening our skills and learning the individual masteries necessary to accomplish our goal.

Mastering the Ancient Arts

The road of trials marks the transition from the beginning of our journey to the middle. The threshold behind us, we are well away on our journey. This section, however, will be the longest portion of our quest from a temporal standpoint. In myth and story, the hero here forges the skills necessary to defeat the enemies he will later face. He or she grows in strength and skill and proves him or herself time and time again. The hero also makes new acquaintances, allies, and enemies during this stage of the journey.

As you seek to step into the fullness of your destiny and accomplish your own heroic goals and legends, you will now need to *do the work* to become the hero you imagine yourself to be. Fully embrace the journey and dive headlong into it, putting the ordinary world behind you. This stage may take time, but you must be willing to go through its difficulties and trials because of the goal at the end of our journey. The work you put in here will later form the basis of the heroic renown you gain in the eye of the bystander.

This is the stage for motivational songs and YouTube videos. It is the stage in which your heart must cry, "Never give up!"

In life, if you set out on a quest that is altogether beyond your ability, you may need to diverge and acquire the skills necessary to accomplish your task. To succeed at such a goal, you will learn, you must have at your disposal an arsenal of skills and abilities. Wisdom, therefore, tells us not to rush headlong into the fight with our arch nemesis or to go straight toward the goal we seek to accomplish.

Instead, have the wisdom and perseverance to make an inventory of those skills you will need in great measure and then gain them one by one until you have achieved such mastery of them on an individual basis that you may weave them together into one grand tapestry.

For example, if I wish to become a renowned writer, I cannot likely just sit down and pen a masterpiece. Instead, I must learn not just how to write but how to produce each individual part of writing with skill and expertise. I must learn plot, structure, dialogue, characterization, and so on. I must pursue each of these skills in measure and mastery before I dare bring them all together into one whole creation. Otherwise, I may do so finding that I have not truly created a masterpiece but instead some half-formed creation devoid of true skill or mastery.

Doing the Work
The purpose of this book is primarily preparatory—it is to prepare you for the journey on which you may embark, if you choose to do anything truly historic or out of the norm.

To succeed on the road of trials, learning is key. In story, especially books, this section is often prolonged. It is a favorite of readers because we relate to this stage so much. It is the section in which the hero learns from a great master. Often the hero fails countless times but always in the safety of the classroom or dojo, where the floors are matted and every failure is rewarded with a gift of insight or instruction from the master. Here it is safe to fail and even necessary. It is only by failing countless times that the hero can approach his final battle with the confidence that he knows how to overcome every possible pitfall and trap of the enemy.

In life, the period of learning is often the bulk of our time spent on the earth and definitely the majority of our time when we are young and still in school.

On your quest to become great, you must understand that during the road of trials, the primary goal is not to pass the trials but to learn the skills that will enable you to defeat your enemy or accomplish your task. The tests or trials are significant only in that they show you whether you are ready to advance to the next stage.

Most often a great hero is assisted in this process of learning by an ascended master—one who has gone before him on the very same quest that he seeks to undertake. For example, Morpheus provides this role for Neo in *The Matrix* when we see Morpheus teaching Neo how to jump across a gap in two buildings or fight in the dojo. If you are able to find a master willing to teach you, you may be able to progress much further along the path than you could otherwise. Additionally, the universe will send a master suited both to your quest and to its gravity. In the case of a truly epic cause, you may need a renowned master of legend.

In life, when you find yourself in this stage, focus on two goals. First, identify clearly those skills you will need to pass your ultimate test and accomplish your quest or mission. Second, devote yourself to study and learning, gaining mastery of the individual skills until you can prove in isolation to have mastered them. Only at that point, when you have shown individual mastery of an array of individual skills, can you move forward a proven warrior on your quest.

Again, looking over the answers to the following exercises, know that as part of your preparation, these skills add into the cost of the undertaking. If you find yourself unwilling to learn some skill absolutely necessary to your quest, you will either need to find a friend or ally to help you or you will likely fail.

Preparation for the Road of Trials
If you can, think ahead to the form your final expression of mastery will take. What will your final battle moment look like? What does it mean for you to accomplish your dream? What skills must you possess in order to achieve victory on your quest? Try to think about them not as a grand display or as a whole but individually. If you are a writer, for example, maybe you need to have a mastery of dialogue, plot, characterization, and so on. If you are an athlete, you must master passing, scoring, and defending in whichever way those skills express themselves in your specific sport. All final battles are a composition of several individual skills, mastered and taken to perfection. By understanding the composite whole now, in advance, you may plan accordingly and prepare for your battle when the day comes.

Do not be greedy and rush headlong to complete your quest. You will be defeated, as sure as the day is light and the night is dark. In that day, your doom will become apparent, and the evil tyrant will laugh over your dead body.

Knowing now the skills you will need, plan how you can master each one of them individually. You may need to seek a wise mentor who is herself a master of these skills. In story, there is usually just one mentor or wise old master. In life, however, you may have a specific professor or teacher for each one of a variety of skills. As you begin to learn them, keep your vision or goal in mind. Know that the hard work you put in now will lead to victory and success later in life.

If you have already started out, you may realize that you possess mastery of one or two skills but are lacking in one or two others. In that case, bring those skills up to their required level, or seek out a friend or ally who can supplement you in your quest. You will need to find a way to fill that gap, somehow.

Enjoy this stage, because death is not currently at your doorstep. Although learning can be hard, a failure here and there as you learn and grow is to be expected—it is part of the process. Only ensure that you are learning from your failures now so that they may not be repeated when the real challenge or trial comes your way. On that day, failure to adequately perform could spell your doom and mean failure for your quest.

You can always start over in life, but starting over can be difficult and painful. If you must, you will be forced to go all the way back to the beginning of the journey and go through once more the stages you have already accomplished until you reach again the place where you failed. Try not to allow this to happen. Instead, be wise and make all the necessary preparations before you start out.

7

MEETING WITH THE GODDESS

Glad for the reprieve from the monk's harsh training, the boy returned to his assigned room in the temple to rest. However, as he did, he looked out and saw below the form of one of the temple attendants on the grounds. Her robes curved around her slim figure, and the sun danced off locks of curly auburn hair.

As she turned, he saw her face and recognized her as the girl who had lifted him from the mud and dirt when he arrived at the temple. Rushing down the stairs and out into the temple grounds at once, the boy called out to her.

She turned to him, the full beauty of her face on display. Her smile was kind, her eyes graciousness itself.

"You seek to become the ascended master?" she asked.

"I do," the boy said.

With a crack of lightning, the sky darkened at once, and the girl seemed to grow large in the boy's sight. Her hair lifted into the air with supernatural power, and her eyes now flashed dangerously.

"Many have attempted to become the ascended master," her voice thundered. "For wealth, for fame, for self. All have failed. Why do you think you will be any different?"

The boy quaked within, but outwardly he fought not to betray the fear.

"My family needs my help. If I fail, they will be lost."

For a moment more, the girl, now a vision of fright, stared into the boy's eyes. He stared back at her, however, and then, as quickly as the storm had come, it dispersed. The girl's hair fell in golden locks around her shoulders, and once more her eyes spoke of grace unmeasured.

"Then I give you a gift, to aid you in the trials to come." With that she drew near and embraced the boy, kissing him on the lips before he could react or withdraw.

As her lips touched his and he felt the soft sensation of her body embracing him, the boy seemed to melt within. The valley of his family, the dark men, the mountain pass, and the trials of the temple all faded. All that remained was the bliss of the embrace and the desire to give such love away to the world.

Calm before the Storm

Like a crucible for your soul, when you arrive at this stage you will have grown from the challenges and trials the universe set out before you. Now, passing unscathed from the trials, the universe will bestow its blessing upon you. Both material success and a natural desire to give love to the world are the result of the meeting with the goddess. Here the universe will bless you, as if with a kiss. And as we will see, your heart will be transformed to give unselfishly to the world.

The stage of meeting with the goddess is portrayed in movies and stories as an embrace between the hero and heroine just prior to the final push or battle. Often the hero has slowly and gradually come to the realization of his love for the heroine. The hero, who up until this point has been the epitome of strength and masculinity, finally shows a tender, gentler side—awakened by the power of love. In her embrace, he is changed to a more giving, loving individual. He learns gentleness, and this transformation of love allows him to carry a new strength of purpose and meaning onto the battlefield of destiny.

It is that tender moment of beauty and love, in the face of the greatest adversity, that spurs the hero on to final victory. It is this meeting with the goddess that gives the hero that required unselfish drive to do what is best for the world, even if it means sacrificing himself. For indeed, the gift of the goddess is worth the price of death.

Love Not Lust

In Joseph Campbell's retelling of this motif, he relies on the story of Acteon and Diana from Greek mythology. I will relate the story in a very similar way to his retelling, as follows.

Acteon was a hunter, a young male, and one day he decided to leave his hunting party, with his companions and his hunting dogs, and wander out alone. After a while he came to a thick grove—the grove of the goddess Diana—and forced his way in. Within the grove there was a grotto, and in the grotto the goddess was bathing naked with her nymphs attending to her, pouring water on her body and washing her.

Seeing the goddess naked, the boy stood and watched, taking in the sight. Immediately the nymphs, out of duty to the goddess, dove to cover her body with theirs. Diana, however, realizing the boy had seen her naked form, stood tall and proud.

"So you have seen me naked," she said, and grabbing what she could threw water in the boy's eyes. "Then tell the world what you have seen, if you can!"

The water splashes the boy, and he is transfigured at once into the form of a stag. He grows antlers and hooves, his legs and arms turn into the legs of a deer, and suddenly he finds himself on all fours. A moment later, he hears his own hunting hounds baying in the distance.

At first he is glad to hear them, but suddenly he takes flight, fear filling his heart. As the story goes, his own hounds hunt him down. He tries to call out and order them to stop, but his vocal cords have morphed and are now incapable of expressing human speech. His dogs attack, tearing him down, and moments later his hunting companions and friends arrive on the scene to deal the final wounding blow, triumphant in their victory over what they perceive to be nothing more than a normal stag.

His is a type of meeting with the goddess, but instead of reacting out of unselfish love, the boy Acteon responds in selfish lust. The symbolism of this story is clear—when we take the gift of the goddess for our own selfish desire, it can and will destroy us.

On the other hand, the Hero who meets with the goddess unselfishly, with a pure heart, will receive the full grace of her ability to give life to the world. This transformative energy will be the basis for the hero's growing supernatural power.

On the foundation of the strength and mastery of skill laid in the road of trials, the meeting with the goddess adds to the hero his or her first transformative gift. The hero who is able to receive from the goddess unselfishly will find a new power in the world—a power to speak, to command. It is an energy capable of turning heads, of captivating audiences, and it is of utmost importance to one who wishes to be truly heroic.

The Greatest Gift

The woman as goddess is the scene in which the hero and heroine finally understand their love for each other and accept their wedding. For us, on this journey of life, it represents the transition between selfish motivation and unselfish, other-focused motivation. At all times in life, we are giving of ourselves to the world. By our very existence on this planet, we affect our surroundings, whether for good or bad.

Realizing this requires a level of maturity from us. It means that we acknowledge the places in life that, in the past, we have selfishly taken from the world. On the other hand, it also frees us to understand more deeply our relationship with the world around us. From this perspective, we may learn to give of our selves to the world. This is the heart of true creation.

The ego represents that idea that separates oneself from our surroundings. When we think about 'I' and 'me' and 'mine', we are living from a delusional perspective. The truth is that we are constantly deeply connected to the world around us. And just as there is life in our bodies, so there is life in all the world around us.

Joseph Campbell tells another story about three brothers who each try to seek out water from a woman who guards a well. The woman appears to be an old hag, winkled and ugly. The first brother goes to her and asks her for some water. She responds that if the boy will give her a kiss, she will fill his water jar. The boy refuses to kiss her, and returns to his brothers thirsty. So the second boy goes as well, and seeing her ugliness, responds that he would rather die of thirst than give the old hag a kiss. Finally, the third brother goes, and he responds that he will not only kiss her, but give her a hug and embrace. They kiss, and immediately she is transformed into the most beautiful girl the boy has ever seen.

Learning to love the world means embracing it for what it is. It means giving love regardless of the appearance the universe presents to you, and understanding that by your unselfish act of giving you transform the world into a more beautiful place. Indeed, through your giving you hold every key necessary to transform the world into your hearts desire.

Having passed the tests and trials and accumulated every skill and resource in our disposal, we descend deeper into the mystical, spiritual nature of our being. In that place we are traverse the streams of life that lead to the mystical marriage with the goddess. From here on, the next several chapters will deal more fully with the psychological battleground we must embrace and overcome if we are to continue on the journey.

Shattering the Ego-Self

By allowing our ego to shatter at the hands of the goddess we blend with her miraculous energy. Refusing to chase union through lust, we become masters of peaceful creation. This union is a sacred moment in our life journey. It is a moment when the victories we have won along the way form the basis for the supernatural strength to be gained, and the touch of the goddess now rests on our physical mastery. Here we are rewarded with the mystical grace to carry our strength into the world through gentle love.

This blessing by the the giving aspect of our nature inspires creative power within. If we are disharmonious with the creative energy within us, instead of transforming our world we will end up destroying ourselves. The selfish, infantile ego seeks only to take; however, when the ego meets with the goddess, it seeks to take that which cannot be taken, the divine grace itself, and is destroyed. The hero, therefore, must allow his own ego to be shattered and pass away so he can receive new grace to give to the world.

An unselfish desire to give from the strength and skill acquired previously now marks the hero. The hero's motives are transformed—a quest begun from selfish motivation must now shift to a more altruistic cause. It is reformed, given new perspective by the light of the goddess's grace.

This stage is highly spiritual, and language used to describe it will clearly ring as strange to the unenlightened mind. The work done here is inward, focused on the shattering of the self-perspective to make room for the unselfish giving perspective. The energy of the goddess inspires creation. It enlivens the skill and strength acquired by the hero on the road of trials.

From this fountainhead of grace, the hero can now create like never before.

Preparation for the Meeting with the Goddess
This meeting often requires a shift in our thought processes. Think about your original goal you set at the outset of this

journey. As you do, look deeply at your motives. Begin to understand that the goodness you bring into the world will truly, deeply affect the lives of all it touches. The effect you have on others will be determined by the motivation you bring with you on the quest.

If your goals are completely self-serving or self-centered, they will come with all sorts of trials and opposition along the way. You will likely destroy yourself under their weight, and if you do meet with success, you will likely end in ruin. Think of all the pop idols we have seen rise to such heights of fame only to crumble under the weight of their popularity. Drugs, alcohol, erratic behavior in the public spotlight—fame is too much for the intact ego-self to take.

It must either shatter of its own choosing or manifest destruction in the external world. Simply put, the intact ego-self is not worthy of the grace of the goddess. You, however, are worthy, if you allow your motivation and deciding factors to shift completely from self to other.

In every quest or goal, there is an underlying current of serving the world. For the true hero, he finds in this stage that he is not only pursuing his quest for his own selfish ambitions but to save the world from persecution and tyranny. At this point, his motivations change, he grows and matures as a hero, and we as an audience suddenly see him in a new light.

It may be difficult to admit at first how self-serving you have been, but the shift is one into a better, higher personality. Allow it to come. Understanding all of this, how can you reorder your motivations to be more giving? In what ways can you sacrifice yourself on this quest in order to benefit the world, so that you may grow into the hero you truly wish to be?

8

WOMAN AS TEMPTRESS

Later, having returned to his quarters to rest, the boy lay awake, staring at the ceiling. He felt light, the memory of the girl's soft touch still lingering on his lips. As he lay there, however, his room darkened. A heavy weight lay on his chest, and dread now filled his heart without reason.

"She felt nice, didn't she?" a soft, sensuous voice said through the darkness.

Lurching upright, the boy stared across his room. There at the edge of the door stood a woman, clad in a revealing satin dress the color of dark blood.

"Who are you?" the boy asked.

"Me?" the woman asked, a smile on her lips. "I am love itself."

Her words dripped with lust, as if to entice the boy into her arms, and she took a single sensuous step toward him.

"How did you get in here?" the boy demanded.

"How? It matters not how, my dear boy, but why. I have come to offer you eternal pleasure. Come!"

The woman took another step forward, and for a moment, the boy was tempted to embrace her, to feel again the softness of a woman's touch. A glint of steel flashed from behind her back the next moment, however, and the spell was broken. At once the boy seized his sword from the dresser and lunged forward, even as the temptress sprung toward him to attack, dagger now raised high.

Caught on his blade, she lurched to a standstill above the boy and, with a cough of blood on her lips, began to writhe in pain.

First her skin darkened. Its lustrous hue turned to pale, grotesque skin. Then her facial features trans- figured as sparkling eyes turned to empty pits of dark- ness. Her dress became at once a thick mat of fur, and leathery wings sprung from her back.

Dropping from the sword, she lay on the floor, dead, her true form revealed.

How Bad Do You Want It?

Success. Fortune. Grace.

In the last stage you experienced your first taste of real success on your journey. The goddess's embrace. You were granted a gift, or even been blessed with some form of material success. However, now temptation will invariably seek you out to destroy you. This stage is dangerous, and if it catch- es you unaware has all the power to stop you in your tracks. If you fall here to temptation, your quest could very well end.

This stage introduces those temptations that threaten to tear us down. Failure to surpass the challenges of this stage is what sets apart "one-hit wonders" from lifetime greats. The temptations and trials of this stage, while pleasurable, distract us from our focus and weaken our spirit, sometimes killing us altogether, other times simply preventing us from continuing on the path we have begun. Although we met with some degree of success, we come to a short end and can proceed no further.

Feminism, an Aside

I would like to briefly address the drastic changes in culture that have taken place over the last half century. *The Hero with a Thousand Faces* was written in 1949, just after the end of World War II and a decade before the civil rights movement would spark in the United States.

In that time, and throughout history, woman was seen as an enigma. At once the giver of life and creation as well as the defeat of countless men at her sometimes-sensuous hands. In the previous chapter, we see her addressed as goddess. Now, in stark contrast, temptress.

I beg you, if you have some strong passions regarding femininity in the twenty-first century, to look past the symbols and instead investigate what they meant at the time of their creation. The meaning behind the symbol still possesses vast value to humanity, and it does so in a nonsexist way. Temptation can come to us in any form—for example, at the end of this book, I outline a journey to getting healthy. On that journey, Cookie and Pizza are the tempters.

So while in *The Hero with a Thousand Faces* the woman takes the role for this fall, in reality she is only a symbol that points to temptation itself, which comes in many forms and must decidedly be overcome on nearly any journey in life—at least if one intends to do anything great.

With that addressed, let us carry on.

Significance of the Temptress

There may be some overlap between this stage and the preceding—it may appear before or directly on the heels of the meeting with the goddess. What is important to understand is that this kind of energy sits in direct opposition to the life force–giving meeting with the goddess. It seeks to dethrone the hero before he ever takes his place, forcing him back from an other-centered state of mind into a taking, self-centered state.

With the hero having attained union with the goddess and receiving the creative energy, temptation now comes to distract and ultimately destroy him. Again, I will harken back to Isaac Newton's third law of motion, which seems so apt in so many places along this journey. The hero must know and understand that for every good attained, there will be some negative energy discharged to match—we have the opportunity, however, to apply our energy to dismiss the negative and embrace the positive. Doing so, we can increase in realms and levels of glory.

The hero must casually—not angrily or in a frustrated manner—turn the temptress aside. It is the role of the hero to move past the temptations of adulterous, lecherous life and go directly toward the heart of the matter. The world and the flesh will naturally call back to the hero, as if to drag him down to death and despair. This tempting is the world system's final attempt to prevent you from meeting with your destiny and defeating the enemies both within and without, to keep you from being able to maintain the focus and clarity required to complete your task.

Furthermore, the lust-driven earthly temptress stands in stark contrast with the heavenly goddess of creativity and grace with whom the hero has mated. She seeks to call him back to his old ego-self, to cause him to reembrace his self-seeking, egotistical nature. From that position the hero will lack the necessary other-centered ability to give and care for the cosmos. If he falls, he will be sapped of the power to defeat the darkness and the enemies at bay and will be utterly destroyed—if not by her, then surely by his enemies when the fateful moment comes.

On a more practical level, when you give in to temptation, you lose sight of what is important. Unvirtuous acts have a way of blinding us. They prevent us from seeing what is important. They weaken our bodies and minds of the spiritual energy we need to disrupt the darkness and create truly good things in life. When you fall into immorally, you handicap yourself when the day of battle comes—and if you have fallen far enough, your immorality may spell the end of your journey.

Whether you are male or female, temptation comes to us all. Understanding this, and that on this quest we seek union and harmony with the giving energy, not obsession with the self-absorbed ego, prepare yourself for the temptation when it comes. By so doing, you will be mentally prepared to pass the test and move into the next stage of realization.

Overcoming Personal Vice

In life, the greatest temptations often come just before or just after some of our greatest successes. Temptation can be toward any vice—not purely sexual, although that is typically what we see in myth and common stories. We give in to our vices and are destroyed by them when we have no hope, no vision for the future. When life seems too much to bear or when we are perhaps naively going on our way to some grand conclusion, not really knowing where we are going or why.

Clarity of purpose, a defined vison and goal in this regard, is our greatest strength.

No one in life sets out to become an alcoholic. No one says to him or herself, "Well, maybe I will become great by having another drink." The thought is laughable. People do so because they have no clear vision for what *not having a drink* will accomplish in their lives. They have no hope, but even hope alone is not enough. It must be clearly defined hope set on a goal at some future point in time. The trade-off between vice and virtue must be well established.

Throughout this journey, we have spoken of your dream. When temptation comes, it is this dream you must keep in mind—this dream that will give you the strength to say no, today, for a much better yes tomorrow.

Image a scale, like the scale of justice. On one hand sits your dream, your vision or goal. On the other, temptation, vice, pleasure. Every moment, your mind works tirelessly to make decisions, to make trade offs. It constantly seeks to find the best result—the choice that will bring the best outcome in your life. However, this scale is an internal scale. It exists in your mind. Now, according to the degree to which your goal will benefit the world, to that same degree the forces of darkness will send temptations into your mind.

These temptations, on the one hand, will load up the scale. Unfortunately, the other side of the scale belongs to you, and you alone. If you put nothing on it, in your mind, then the temptations sent by the powers of darkness will overwhelm you and you will sink down into moral defeat. However, if you establish within your minds eye the clear vision of your dream accomplished, then by the degree of your understanding you will be able to escape temptation.

The scales of justice will weigh the two, and the greater will prevail. If, having defined your goal, you still find your-self still falling to temptation, realize then that the goal you have set is not nearly heroic enough—not truly worth your life inspiration—because if it were, you would no longer find yourself clamped down by a self-centered existence.

Force Multipliers

If you find yourself unable to overcome the temptations of this stage, one of two things could be happening. Either the value of your goal is not worthy of the trouble it will take to achieve, or you simply must further clarify your 'why' and 'how'.

The answers to the questions at the end of each chap-ter form what I call force multipliers—each one stacking on the last and, instead of adding to, multiplying the effect. Clarifying, for example, who specifically your quest benefits, what wrong will be overturned in the world, and what form your final expression of mastery will take will be strong value propositions that should easily overturn temptation when it comes.

Knowing where you are going, how you will get there, and for whom you will go will be invaluable psychological motiva-tion to keep going. With the true value of the quest revealed, how will you fall to temptation still, knowing that only death awaits?

The scales of justice will, internally, weigh for you whether the goal is worthy of the sacrifice at hand. If the goal is found to be lacking in weightiness, you will fail. On the other hand, if you have understood the various stages of the journey and applied the necessary psychological shifts (for example, tran-sitioning from selfishness to focus on others and discerning who will most benefit from your victory), then you will pass by temptation quickly and without pause or drawn-out conflict.

In regard to these scales, the weight of temptation grows in accordance with the value of the good we hope to bring into the world. Additionally, the level of temptation directed our way does not seem to be in accordance with our *perceived* good—the good we see in our mind—but with the *actual* good we are bringing into the world. This is an extremely important distinction to make.

If there is a large degree of separation between the *perceived* and *actual* good you are creating, that difference could be enough to tip the scales of temptation in the favor of vice rather than virtue. In the kingdom of your mind, the value you perceive is the value you will follow. Let me give an example:

Let's say you set out with the goal to make life better for your husband and two children. You want to make a million dollars so you can buy them a nice house and clothes. OK. Not a bad place to start. You are doing some good in the world.

However, along the way, you realize that to make that million dollars, you are going to need to make the lives of half a million people noticeably better. Unfortunately, you never adjust your dream vision—it still centers on you, your husband, and your two kids. Meanwhile, all the forces of opposition are screaming against you because you are setting out to change the lives of five hundred thousand people. The scales tip, the vision proves unworthy, and temptation and vice rule the day and strike you down.

You have failed. Your dream vision, which was positive and worthy when starting out, no longer measures up to the true good you are bringing into the world. In light of the meeting with the goddess, we can see clearly why: The vision you thought was altruistic was still centered on you and your family. It did not grow, did not change to see the wider group of humanity that in *reality* you were going to benefit.

The Monster Looming

In today's world, we face challenges and problems never before known to humanity. With the invention of the Internet, computers, television, and satellites, the world is more connected than ever before. Information is at our fingertips in ways it never was in the past. Previous generations seem to lack the answers to the challenges we face today: "Why do you not have the answer to my pain? Why are you incapable of solving this huge problem destroying my life, you who claim to have all the answers?"

The reason the leaders of previous generations lack any clear answers to the seemingly insurmountable challenges and temptations our generation faces is because they have never had to overcome these challenges before. Simply put, they never had to rise to the challenges we now face. Ours is a new generation—our problems, our challenges, we are the first to meet them. In this regard, the burden of overcoming these challenges falls squarely on our shoulders. A hero must rise in our generation with the answer, the power to overcome the great tyrants setting out to destroy our lives.

That hero, when he or she (or even they) arises, will bring a battle call to virtue. He or she will possess the sword of justice that will strike the heart of the hidden monster and call all the forces of purity to battle. On that day, the fallen warriors will arise, gifted by the blessing of grace with a shattered ego-self and vision for the benefit of humanity. They will arise

with power in their wings and set out to destroy the great tyrant hidden in their lives.

Their hero, as we will see in the chapter "Apotheosis," will
be the embodiment of their cry—the personification of the
collective call for freedom from the oppression of unmanage-
able temptation.

Preparations for the Temptress

In preparing to overcome temptation, we must first start by
knowing precisely which kinds of temptation we can expect
along the way. First, what are your most common personal
vices or moral failings? You know what they are, for they are
plain as day to you and likely everyone around you. Be sure,
as you push forward on your quest, they will raise their ugly
heads when you are least ready for them. List them now.

Also realize that often the temptation will be directly tied
to the quest. Trying to lose weight? Everyone who has ever
gone on such a journey knows immediately what a great temptation cookies and pizza suddenly become.

Know, however, that as temptations arise, they do so only
to steal and rob from you an eternal treasure that is manifesting in your daily life. You must be prepared for this to happen
by knowing what your goal is and how it will benefit the world.
When temptation of thought and mind arises, you must be
ready with your goal clearly defined and of such value to both
you and society that temptation has no voice.

9

ATONEMENT WITH THE FATHER

The next morning, with the memory of the girl's soft touch now tempered by his encounter with the temptress, the boy descended to the inner cloister of the temple, where the wise old monk awaited him.

He made mention of the encounter to the old man, but the monk only nodded and said, "I see," as if it were nothing new to him, and directed the boy to the entrance of the innermost chamber.

"Within this cloister you will face the darkness itself. Rarely have any come this far along the path. Those who have, without exception, have failed. If you are prepared, I can only open the way. From here on, you will have only your own strength to guide you. Are you ready?"

With a gulp and a brief thought to the battles he had fought so far, the boy nodded. "I am," he said.

The monk, lowering his head, reached to a large lever that protruded from the floor. He pulled it back, and somewhere deep within the temple the noise of grinding machinery could be heard. Before them, a large plate that sat in the wall began to roll to the side, revealing a stairway that descended into darkness.

The monk said not a word but only looked at the boy, and the boy in similar fashion did not break the reverent silence. Instead, summoning all his resolve, the boy stepped down into the darkness below.

When he had gone on for some time, not even the stair beneath his feet visible in the dark abyss, he came to a place where the floor became level ground. Stepping forward, he felt his way through the dark feebly.

Just when he wondered whether anything at all would happen, the floor beneath him shook. Lightning flashed, and he found himself floating in a great expanse, standing on nothingness itself.

The lightning flashed again, and now the boy stood in his father's home in the valley. The boy's father sat at the table, and his mother was busy nearby preparing a meal. At the window the boy's older brother stood, staring out into the fields beyond, where the boy himself sat a long ways off, watching over his flock.

"We can't let him go, Arthur," the boy's mother said from the stove.

"We have no other choice," the father, Arthur, said from his place at the table.

"I can do it," the brother said from the window. "I won't fail you."

"Please," the woman begged.

"Listen to your son, Melissa," Arthur said. "He can save us from the Mascareans. It's either him or..."

"*No, not my youngest. He's still innocent. Leave him out of this.*"

"*Then we have to let James go. It is the only way.*"

"*And allow our eldest to be a minion of the Mascarean Empire?*"

"*What else would you have me do, woman?*" the old man cried. "*My arms are no longer strong enough to carry a bow to battle. We will give them James and let them come to our land. Otherwise we will all perish. We have not the strength to fight them. One day, when the boy is grown, he will understand.*"

The boy, who stood as nothing more than an apparition in the faded memory of the unconscious sublime, felt his heart break within himself. His father had allowed the dark riders into their valley—he had been the one to send his brother to fight for them, to enslave their own people.

The scene dissolved, and once again the boy stood in pitch-black emptiness. A tear fell from his eye into the abyss.

"*What will you do?*" *a voice, strong and thunderous, said from the expanse.*

The boy wiped another tear from his eye.

"*I will fight. I will save them,*" *he said.*

"*But it was your own father who let them come in the first place,*" *the voice responded.*

"*I will do what he could not. He could not save my family. But I will!*"

With that, an energy leaped from the boy's heart and spiraled out into the expanse. Suddenly the place was ablaze with color and wonder.

"Very well, then. Become what your father could not. Save your family!"

Family Matters

You will know yourself to be in the center of an atonement with the father moment in your life if suddenly you realize that the central reason for your dream or quest is a lingering childhood trauma. In metaphor and story, this applies specifically to the hero's father. In life, it can extend to any of the people or social factors that influenced our childhood. Our childhood experiences can have drastic impacts on the way we view life, and the needs our hearts express.

Atonement with the father will heighten your mastery of our world to a plane of soul health, wherein you will surpass physical success alone and reach into the realm of greatness. Here we find those figures who possess both renown and humility—those whom we respect, whom we aspire to become. It is a place of inward healing, a place of complete, focused wholeness that will unleash you on the world to transform and change it in the fullest way possible. It will give you the strength and power to right injustice, to overturn the ways of the world, and to free yourself and those around you from oppression.

Universally, no man takes a place of more central importance in the human psyche than our parents. They gave life to us, protected us, and safeguarded our lives. They defended us when we were young.

Eventually, however, there comes a time in life when the child must take the place of leader in his or her own life. No longer do the parents' voice carry absolute authority over the

HERO

decisions of the child—now the hero arises, knowing that they must accomplish their dream despite the protests of the previous generation. This is a powerful coming of age moment, and the atonement with the father motif discusses that moment in each of our lives when we fully take on the weight of our humanity.

What follows in this chapter may be a shock, if you are not fully prepared for it. Just as the monk in the fable said, few have come this far in the journey—far fewer still have made it through unscathed and completed it. I will introduce it to you directly, so continue reading only if you are fully prepared.

With that in mind, I will ask you:

Are you ready?

The Central Transformation

The whole point of atonement with the father is this: that the failings of the hero's father are the very goads that sparked the need for the quest in the first place. This is often expressed specifically in a father and son motif in story. Symbolically, in your life it could potentially extend to either of your parents or even the environment of your upbringing. You will know when you have entered it because the pain caused will leap directly into your mind.

This is the central element of the drama of life. Some of the greatest power and freedom can only be released when we first realize this and then, staring down the cause of our greatest failure, forgive and remove the tarnished lens from our eyes. Our parents, who commanded us to obey when we were young, represent the last voice of external control over our internal being. To truly transcend, as the hero must, at some point you must overcome these bonds.

Although our parents loved us, they also had failings of their own. And so often, these failings accumulate into a psychological need to transform our world for the better. Truly, our world does need some changing—it is not a perfect place, and there is not a single perfect person in it. However, before we can create our own justice in the external world, we must first find freedom in the inner world of our psyche.

Atonement with the father is attained when we realize that our own personal failings in life—the problems of our life and often the central issue of the quest we have undertaken—are nothing more than the ramifications of our parents' failings.

Through the lens of symbol, we can see that though the hero loves his father so tremendously, he often idolizes him and fails to see his humanity and his failures. Instead of acknowledging what is wrong in him, the hero denies that he could have even a single failing until it is almost too late.

In life, when we do not see the truth of our circumstances, with both the positives and the negatives, we risk recreating the failures of our previous generations. Internally, our subconscious mind knows of these failings, and shows us the path to correcting them through the dream and quest we choose to take when setting out to do something great.

For simplicity sake, I will speak throughout this chapter using the term parents, but know that as your own circumstances in life differ widely, so too will the source of pain or failing. For you, when you read the word parents here, you may want to substitute any person who strongly influenced your childhood, whether for good or bad.

When you understand atonement with the father in the light of our own personal quest or mission—if you have really chosen your life's central calling—things should quickly begin to fall into place. It is in this central state of mind that you may identify that character flaw or internal set of beliefs which have likely caused so much hurt in your life. The next step, of course, is more shocking and difficult than the last. Facing the source of your central pain, you must now forgive and, by so doing, overcome. Forgive and overrule the darkness brought in against your will when you were young.

This is how you heal. When you have succeeded in this quest, you will have overcome some fundamental flaw the previous generation was unable to overturn. Thus we as a human species race ever onward toward greater and greater levels of perfection. Make no mistake, you as well will pass on some failing to your own children—though it is the hope of every mother and father to be a perfect example to their children, we all see only through a glass dimly, or a mirror darkly, into the truth of this life.

Take heart as you look inwardly to yourself and your parents in the thoughts below. Learn to acknowledge your parents failings, where they may exist, without dissolving their victories. It is in both victory and failure that we find the real image of those who came before us in this life.

The Need for Atonement
Atonement with the father is the second sacred union in which we experience a heightened divine connection with the universe. This time the symbol is that of the father, in all his fierce tenacity, that we must face down. The image here is of the thunder and lightning of the depths of the temple, resounding with terror. The lightning that echoes from the throne pours down around us, and we must approach with great tenacity.

Ancient humanity connected the father with god, the creator. From this perspective, the harsh realities of the physical world were deeply entwined with human survival. The wrath of god, the father, was deeply feared. Coming to terms with the world we live in, with creation itself, and with our own parents requires us to grow up. It forces us to assert our own power over the world around us, to stand down the external forces that would run our lives, and to become powerful in our own right.

In our own lives, we all have a coming of age moment. We realize the fallibility of our parents, and learn that we must assert our own authority upon the world. We govern ourselves, we take command of our lives. For the hero, this means standing down the force of nature or the great tyrant their own parents simply could not defeat.

And for you, it may very well take a similar manifestation. In your life, you have set out to fill some deep need left by the failures of a previous generation. This stage is both a moment of realization—recognition for what is really happening in your life—and of triumph, when you decide you truly will fulfill that missing piece.

Able to look now at the holes left in our lives by our parents, either intentionally or unintentionally, we must accept their failures and successes and through forgiveness heal the wound that was inflicted. Then we have the power to create the solution we so desperately desired in the first place. And having done so, we find atonement. We see our parents and society on an even plane, a level playing field, and take our rightful new place in the story of our own lives. We become the creator of our own destiny.

On a cosmic scale, in the inner mystical union, we atone by seeing the heavenly Father for who he truly is. We come to a place of self-acceptance in his eyes and are atoned for. By passing through the flaming spikes of his wrath and fury, we can perceive him through the eyes of self-actualization. When we are one with the Father, we enter a plane of realization wherein our natural limitations as human beings break away and dissolve. Suddenly, we are no longer like the fearful mortals around us but are filled with a courage that comes from our realization of the eternal, indestructible nature of our own souls.

Looking Inward

Personally, we atone with our parents by coming to terms with the life they have given us, and pushing through to create our own reality. Sometimes, this requires deep introspection. For example, we may sometimes find ourselves obsessing over childhood wounds or needs. When these things present themselves, inner healing must take place.

On this journey, the most I can say here is not to run from the pain when it reveals itself. Instead, face it head on. Try to forgive, to overcome, and to allow the pain to wash away. It may be wise, for some, to seek out expert guidance, such as a counselor to help with the healing journey.

Once we have healed, however, we become able to commune with the spirit in and around us. We see the universe clearly, the wounds of our parents resolved. We have defeated our brother and seen his humanity. We have partnered with the creative and divine aspect of the goddess mother, and our ego has shattered. We no longer partner with selfish motivation but instead move to give to the universe.

Entering into the temple of our parent's house, we can face down the terror that haunts us in the night, the wound and fright left by those much more powerful than we were when young. We can overturn the words or even those physical wounds where they may exist and apply the healing balm of the goddess in conjunction with the skill and strength we achieved along the path. The supernatural amulets or aids that helped us initially now prove worthless in the face of these inner wounds—but we no longer need them. We ourselves are now strong enough to go head-to-head with the wrath that lingers and cast aside those toys to embrace the fullness of our humanity and destiny.

At the end of the fight, which for us is more of a healing process, we emerge victorious—now at one with the father spirit in the world, able to create and govern. Free from the wounds placed on us, we see the true nature of our deity. We are one with the creator. Our perspective shifts, and the dark thunders of the creator's wrath give way to clear skies and light of day.

Preparations for Atonement with the Father
To find true internal peace, we must heal the wounds our parents left on us when we were children. This can be a painful and difficult process to go through. The wounds you may find within yourself are deep and have existed for years or decades. They are clung to, cherished as central aspects of your identity by this point in time.

Know that what you are doing here is of central importance to your ability to accomplish your life dream. You must first heal the wounds and scars on the inside which have manifested outwardly in your life circumstances. This is the only way you will have the psychological strength to transform your circumstances in the external world when the time comes.

Your subconscious mind will not allow you to venture deeper than you are prepared to go. The assistance of a trained counselor is of vast import. Depending on your individual circumstances in life, it may be very advisable that you seek one out. Some are more spiritual than others, and in certain cases you may be advised to seek licensed, professional help.

If you do seek to undergo this transformation personally, know that you will be forced to heal those wounds which brought you to this point. When they are revealed, it is of the upmost importance that you forgive the offender. Although this chapter is entitled "Atonement with the Father," the wounds of childhood and life can come from any direction, and unless forgiven and healed from, fester and breed destruction in our lives. As you think about your childhood and images arise, forgive the offender for any pain they inflicted on your soul.

10

APOTHEOSIS

The universe spiraled before the boy, vast and wondrous. Below he saw his world, his planet, his family, and the families of all the others hidden in the valley of his home. On the horizon the dark hordes now descended on the valley, burning buildings and killing many of those they came in contact with.

When a family stood on their doorstep, dark bandana in hand, painted with the red circle of the Mascarean Empire, that house the riders passed by, acknowledging their surrender. But where a man took up shield or sword against the riders, there five men for every one fell on the resistors, impaling and killing any who didn't comply.

Before the boy, his father stood with his mother by his side and raised in his hand the black-and-red bandana of the Mascareans. With a sneer, the faceless rider passed them by, as if resentful of losing the chance to wet his spear with their blood. The bandana, the boy now knew, purchased by the blood of his eldest brother.

Suddenly pain and anger erupted from the boy's heart, gushing outward like fire on the scene. His hair stood on end, and energy engulfed his body like a blanket and, with a shout, exploded outward, wiping the entire scene away as it did.

"No!" the boy yelled, crying out into the cosmos.

Now all the energy of the galaxy was at his fingertips. He could feel the rush of power, and suddenly he no longer was himself. Filled with cosmic energy, his mind transformed. Beyond good and evil, beyond his mother and father, he simply was.

He was the energy of the universe. He was the light that would dispel the darkness.

The hero was born.

The Chosen One

The energy of the cosmos rushes in on you. You feel the power of the divine. Your personal ego has been wiped away, and you now focus on completing your quest from a divine, entirely whole perspective. You have attained what is known as apotheosis.

Apotheosis is a motif that runs as a theme throughout many stories where the central element is transformation. The word literally means "to be elevated to the status of God." If you have ever believed that you are special, chosen for some great purpose, or set apart, apotheosis is the stage in which that chosen quality explodes into reality. It is the point in the story where the divine takes on flesh—or, alternatively, when the human ascends to the realization of godhood. From this vantage point, the hero is now able to defeat the darkness that had terrified the entire world.

When you experience apotheosis, you will feel the power of God rushing through your body, the spirit of the universe compelling you forward. The justice of the world will become your driving force. Your quest will be absolved into something greater, your destiny now intrinsically tied to humanity or society as a whole.

This third reckoning goes beyond the plane self and other and represents a spiritual union in which we attain a level of realization comparable to the spiritual greats of history. Where in previous stages of the mystical union we transcended the limits of self and healed from the wounds of our past, we now move beyond the familial designations of the infantile consciousness and into the nameless void.

In this third and final mystical union, we build on our healing union with self and other by totally, completely transcending personal limitation. Here we move into the all-encompassing void of the entire universe. The nameless, faceless void, wherein we become truly one with all creation. In this state of apotheosis, we realize our bodies, made of molecules of matter, are nothing more than the composite holding cells for our local consciousness, presently and only momentarily separated from the great eternal mind from which all creation sprung. In this state of being, our personal consciousness dissolves into a sea of ego death, and we spread our mind out among the cosmos. This is the final, highest state of mystical union.

What Is the Apotheosis?
I am going to create a new word here. *Apotheotical.* It doesn't exist. Not a word.

It is now. The definition of *apotheosis* is "elevation to divine status: deification," from the *Merriam-Webster* dictionary.

Apotheosis is the moment of the hero's life wherein he or she is raised to a level equivalent with God.

Apotheosis is God taking on the human form—elevating a hero to divine status so that the hero in question, who has proven him or herself through countless trials and challenges, may now take on some tyrant so powerful that none other than God him/herself could destroy it. It is the moment—the apotheotical moment—when all the collective cries of the universe for freedom from some specific oppression collect in a divine answer. And that answer, surprisingly, comes not in the form of a lightning bolt from heaven but in a man or woman possessed of the power to destroy the demon itself.

The hero, having attained both union with the goddess and atonement with the father, is now deemed fit by that force of awe-inspiring creative power that ultimately transcends all human limitations of self and other. This almighty rushing spirit puts the hero on, and the hero now himself transcends. It is no longer he who speaks—no longer he who acts.

He takes on an altogether different persona—that of God himself. That gift that so countless many would have taken out of selfish ambition—to become one with God—is now granted to the hero who has fully divested himself of ego-self so as to make room for the divine persona.

The energy of the universe culminates in the hero's body. He hears the cries of the oppressed—his heart breaks. But now, instead of being overwhelmed by the intensity of their cries, the energy of the Almighty rushes forth with the power to destroy the yoke of oppression. His voice thunders—his spirit is lightning.

He speaks now not from a place of self but from a position of almighty empowerment. He is the one who will destroy the

tyrant. He is the one who will free his people. God is willing
to humble himself for such a one—to take on the hero's flesh
to save and free his creation that he loves so dearly.

This is the apotheotical moment. This is apotheosis.

Experiencing Apotheosis Firsthand

These kinds of universal, nonpersonal realizations are the
much sought after treasure of many mystical traditions worldwide. From Mother Teresa experiencing the ecstasy of god
through her love for the poor orphans in India, to Siddhartha
Gautama experiencing the eternal bliss of enlightenment,
apotheosis is the peak of many supernatural experiences.

Whether sought after in the cloister of the monastery or
temple, or experienced firsthand through the ego-breaking
revelations that accompany great trials and perseverance in
the face of oppression, this state of enlightenment reveals to
the hero a truth far greater than the world of common, every
day appearance. The world of quantum physics, now so en-
grained in popular culture, seems to speak of the same mysteries. It is to the initiate who has passed the trials and entered
this state of enlightened bliss that revelation comes firsthand.

In ancient culture, this experience formed the basis for
the transition from initiate to master or from youth to adult.
It was often central to coming of age rites which took place in
many tribal cultures. Experiencing apotheosis grants us the
ability to perceive the world from a new perspective, to detach
from emotional and intrapersonal cares and concerns and
move toward an experience of transcendent peace.

Entire tomes and religions have been devoted to seeking
out this kind of religious experience. At the height of many

myths of the world, apotheosis is an experience every human should taste at least once in his or her lifetime. Despite this, however, it remains far beyond the bounds of a complete description in this kind of book.

Stories that feature this kind of realization also often take on specific themes that tend to revolve around the apotheotical truth that will be revealed to the hero at the climax of the story. So powerful is this theme that when it does present itself, the entire story world seems to revolve around the experience and the supernatural power and authority to be gained from it.

Preparations for Apotheosis

Like the chosen one, called from birth for a single, world changing goal, the experience and transformation that takes place in the apotheotical moment has been heralded as the mark of a savior, and it will be so for you as well as you step into your destiny and call. Everything up to this point in the journey has been leading you inextricably towards this destination. Less to be prepared for or thought about, and more to be embraced and experienced firsthand when it comes, this stage will literally transform your very nature.

Do not fight this experience, when it comes. It will give you the power and perspective to transform your reality in the most radical, life changing of ways. You will come into a state of total realization of self and reality. You will be introduced directly to your transcendental self.

When that time comes, the limitations will dissolve. They will fall off and fly away. You will be more free than ever before. You will know your power, and your strength, and you will have the strength of the universe to propel you forward. You will transcend into an experience of divine empowerment to do your duty to the world. Do not resist this experience of cosmic consciousness melting—it is for the good of all humanity.

11

ULTIMATE BOON

The hero stood now on a platform of gold. In his furious energy, he had hardly noticed as the platform formed beneath his feet. On either side a column of gold rose into the ether, and before him, quite a ways along the platform, there rose a great pedestal of gold. Atop the pedestal sat a large spherical vase filled with a sparkling blue liquid.

Above, wings of light materialized like angels, and a thousand eyes suddenly opened to stare down on him, each the size of a human body. The form of the great beyond would have terrified the boy—but it was no longer the boy who stood in that place. It was the hero.

"Take the vial," the voice thundered. "Within it is the elixir of life—once the darkness is destroyed from your land, break the contents over the valley and the light will return."

The thousand eyes blinked strangely above, and the hero walked forward to the pedestal. Mounting the stairs, he reached up and took the spherical flask from its shelf.

The Elixir of Life

Your ultimate boon stage will come when, having tapped into the transcendent and transformative energy, you are now able to create a great masterpiece. Whether a work of art or a masterful performance on the field or stage, your ultimate boon represents the sought after prize. It is your magnum opus, or "great work".

It is that masterpiece of art, literature, or sportsmanship that can put on display, through the human vessel of clay, a supernatural grace that transcends the limitations of the physical world. When the work must be done in private prior to a public revealing, it will coalesce in the place the universe calls the ultimate boon.

This final type of realization expresses itself as the state of flow we enter when we achieve such mastery of our art that we access a semi-timeless state, perceiving motion and action on another level of reality and granting us the power to achieve ultimate success in some act or contest. This level of mastery may be achieved through the culmination of the path set out in the preceding pages. It is worth noting that this state of flow is a much-heralded and sought-after state of ultimate mastery. There are no shortcuts to achieving it. Attaining it requires both immeasurable practice and also the emotional and spiritual transformations we have discussed. However, understanding this path may at least speed your ability to attain it on your path.

Go with the Flow

The ultimate boon is the promised reward on our journey. It is the ultimate, final enabler that allows us to produce a masterpiece of artwork, perform at the level of a Michael

Jordan, speak with such wisdom entire religions form around our words, or lead social movements that radically transform society.

It is described as the state of flow, that state of such mastery where we enter into a moment-by-moment conscious experience of the present, wherein our ability to control our own bodies and the movements or thoughts we produce is heightened dramatically.

Flow, or the ultimate boon, as it is referred to in myth and legend, is the culmination of a lifetime of work to focus and direct the entirety of the human psyche toward one singular aim. It is the reward of the master who has challenged the gods and all the powers that be, come to a complete and dramatic realization of self, healed the entirety of his body and mind, and set forward to change the course of human history entirely through his actions and triumphs.

Here is the great master born. The legend, the myth himself, the hero who is at the center point of our story. When you have attained this level of self-realization, you are able to produce and create on par with any historical figure of your craft. The ultimate boon is the goal we have sought—it is the result for which this book was written.

The Tangible Boon
The ultimate boon is the tangible reward or proof of the journey of transformation. When the world is physically lacking some cure, for example, the ultimate boon may take the form of that healing draught. A scientist, perhaps, could search for the cure to a great disease and find in the ultimate boon the much-desired chemical compound that dispatches the plague once and for all. Notice, however, that simply finding the cure

is not enough—it is not the end of the quest. The scientist must still bring his cure to the world and ensure the forces of opposition do not prevent the cure from seeing the light of day.

In another example, the ultimate boon could be a book that synthesizes perfectly the answer to much-asked questions of humanity.

I hope, in some small way, to have contributed to your finding it. Hopefully you and many others will come into possession of this ultimate boon, this highest level of realization, and together we will transform humanity from its current state into one more glorious and beautiful. The point here is that this transformation will come only when we all together have healed our wounds, conquered our own personal giants, and allowed our ego-selves to be shattered by the giving touch of the mother goddess. And when, through mastery of skill, we are able to take everything we have learned and express it through craft or trade, then humanity will be healed in its entirety.

The Hidden Treasure of the Gods
The ultimate boon in story is often described as "guarded by the Gods themselves." Kept in the temple of the gods, it appears as if the divine forces seek to prevent this ultimate boon from ever reaching humanity's hands. From time immemorial, they have kept it hidden. They do so even till this day. It is the elixir of life, the fountain of youth, the spring of immortality.

The gift, however, is extremely delicate. In the wrong hands, horrible tragedies could be caused to manifest. The elixir itself, exposed to even the slightest impurity, could be destroyed and lost forever, never to be recreated again. The gods guard the way to the ultimate boon for this reason: to prevent an unstable, immature humanity from grasping, for there is only one of every specific boon, and in the wrong hands, it can be destroyed.

The elixir of life, it turns out, is a very delicate thing—able to give immortality but also at once ruined by the slightest impurity. "Who can ascend on high?" the psalmist asks and responds, "He who has cleans hands and a pure heart." Why? Because even a little impurity can spoil the whole batch. For any dream, any quest, there is some fulfillment, some creation or masterpiece to be achieved. The ultimate boon represents that masterpiece, hidden deep within the collective unconscious of humanity, waiting to be discovered.

The gods turn out to be guarding the ultimate boon not because they do not want humanity to seize it—but because they do not want humanity to lose its one chance at eternal life. In the story of the hero, the ultimate boon may be a gift capable of finally defeating the tyrant who has brought destruction and terror to the land. However, if one unprepared to defeat that tyrant were to seize the gift, that person would be destroyed in the final battle, the gift either lost or—worse yet—claimed by the tyrant himself to further enslave humanity.

Everything in the journey has purpose. Every step along the way has been measured. You may not seize your ultimate boon before you are ready, for in doing so, you would risk destroying yourself and making the world not a better place but, in fact, a darker place by far.

Preparations for the Ultimate Boon
Like other revelations about spirit and self, the ultimate boon cannot directly be prepared for. Instead, it is the culmination

of countless hours of hard work and dedication combined with the psychological readiness that presents itself when the spirit is whole. At the same time, however, it can be envisioned. Many athletes who are exceptional in their sports help their subconscious mind enter this state more easily by completing visualization exercises.

To do so, they see themselves perfectly and fluidly going through the motions of their sport. In their quiet moment of reflection, they watch as they sink the perfect dunk, make the perfect pass, and so on. Doing so aids them when the time comes to perform on the court or field. Self-visualization has been proven to be a powerful tool for entering into altered states of consciousness. Take some time to see and feel yourself succeeding or achieving victory in your chosen arena.

Of course, this exercise of visualization cannot and should not take the place of real training. It is only the ultimate boon on top of the actual physical mastery of the sport or skill itself. The visualization forms the final layer—when on the court, having perfectly executed all game long and displayed consistently one maneuver of skill after the next, now the ultimate boon can express itself in the game-winning shot that should have been impossible even for the greatest athlete.

When the ultimate boon comes, if you are creating a work of art or some masterpiece, embrace it and dive in headlong. In this case, think about what form it could take, and use that final form as inspiration to go on. If you seek to produce in your quest a magnum opus, what form will it take?

ACT THREE

The Return

This final section regards the transition back to the real—the world around us so often refuses to change at the pace with which we change. Any first-timer on this path will be met with extreme difficulty as she returns to the world of her friends and family for the first time, finding them painfully *unchanged.* Understanding this section will empower you to bring the realizations attained in the previous section back into the world, thus accomplishing outward change. Ultimately, this stage completes the cycle, leading back to the beginning and once again calling to the hero to undergo a quest of transformation and change.

At this point in the guide, I wish to impart some inspiration to continue the quest through multiple cycles of transformation. Intuitively, I can tell you that completing the entire cycle over time, on both macro and micro cycles, will reward you with victories that grow in scale organically. For example, in nature, plants and some animals quite often grow according to a mathematical sequence known as the Fibonacci sequence. This sequence builds on itself, starting out small but over time making larger and larger leaps. After a short while, the sequence seems to explode out of control.

Take a plant, for instance, which will start out as a small seed, and slowly sprout. As it grows, however, its branches suddenly become larger and larger, until it takes the form of a full-grown tree. Another example is that of the seashell, which starts as a small, tightly wound vessel whose outer hull eventually grows much larger than all the inner sections together.

Though at first you may see only small rewards here and there from your endeavors, if you continue on the journey over a period of time, you will see the results start to grow.

Soon, victories will begin to explode (figuratively speaking) in your life. A journey that started as a small seed will grow to a small sprout, and over time will become an incredible tree in your life. Greater and greater accomplishments will unfold before your eyes. You will do things you never dreamt of, things once far beyond your ability to achieve.

Though you may encounter greater trials with each iteration, you will be stronger each time, and as you progress, you will no doubt make a name for yourself as a world hero, one of the greats of humanity. I only hope that by that time, enough will have read this work that a new era of humanity will begin, in which heroes outnumber those who are average or normal among us, and great transformation can come to our species.

Manifesting the Outer Palace
In the following pages, you will read about the final stages of the hero's journey. By the time you actually arrive at this stage, however, it is very likely that a large amount of time will have passed between the reading of this book—this road map—and the arrival at your destination. These final chapters, therefore, are both a description of that landing zone and an encouragement to arrive there. The final tests in this third section of the journey symbolize the outward manifestation of the inner transformation that took place in the preceding section.

They are, therefore, cumulative of the steps one must take to transition from inner seeker to outward master of reality. It is in this section that those skills acquired in the road-of-trials stage will be put into outward physical practice.

If the initiate into the divine mysteries foolishly rushed ahead into mystical ecstasy, such as the meeting with the goddess, atonement with the father, or apotheosis, without mastering some outward skill, he would find a painful requirement to return to the road-of-trials phase and start again as a student. Now a master of inner mystery, he would be forced to humble himself and learn once more the physical tools and skills that would aid him in manifesting outwardly that inner knowledge. In this case, rather than becoming a student again, the devotee often is forced into a prolonged or even permanent refusal-of-the-return stage—because he has no real tool to outwardly manifest the newly acquired inward knowledge, a return would mean only death.

In the case of reality, having attained transcendent knowledge without any skill by which to display its applicability, the devotee is forced to render into words that which is much better displayed through action. Then, with the words having fallen on deaf ears, the seeker feels the rushing pain of defeat. On the other hand, if the seeker has acquired mastery of a set of physical skills prior to attaining absolute enlightenment of the soul, the universe seems to conspire to rush him to the point of destination. This is seen in the chapter "Magic Flight."

The most important point of this final section, and really the climax of the story, is contained in the chapter "Master of the Two Worlds." The goal of reading this book, of course, is not to read the climactic chapter but to prepare for your own personal achievement or victory in life. It is to focus all your energies toward one clearly attainable goal and, equipped with the knowledge of all the challenges, pitfalls, and requirements along the way, speed directly to that victory. Therefore, the "Master of the Two Worlds" chapter will not only describe what awaits here but revisit the clear vision and preparation for it. Completing the exercises at the end of the chapter may inspire you to revisit the chapter "Road of Trials" and more clearly define which skills will be required during your own final battle.

After succeeding in becoming master, the final battle complete, victory achieved, the last chapter focuses on the aftermath. "Freedom to Live" simply describes what awaits the victor, the hero, his or her task accomplished. I hope it may prove further motivation to complete the quest, although the highest motivation is not the reward but the transformation of reality that comes through the victory itself.

12

REFUSAL OF THE RETURN

Standing on the pedestal, flask in hand, for a moment the hero paused. "How nice it would be," he thought briefly, "to stay in this hall of golden power for all eternity." As if to appease him, the wings and eyes above stayed silent, did not move to interfere.

The thought of his family, however, returned to the hero's mind, and at once he resolved himself to return.

The Way Back

Having mastered the four fundamental transformations and gained the mastery to change the world, you must now return to it. Some, however, long to stay forever in that state of mystical enlightenment which was gained in the inner corridors of the mind and heart. This is the refusal of the return stage. If you find yourself in it, you may not wish to return to the real world at all, but rather stay hidden in the spiritual ecstasy discovered within.

This begins in earnest what is called the return, which starts with our natural inclination not to return to the world of the norm—to remain in the bliss of the heavenly abode forever. The difficulties and struggles of *normal life* seem so trivial to us that we refuse to embrace them as even real. The great religions of the world express that this is not necessarily a mistake. However, it represents a more selfish decision to stay in the state of eternal bliss rather than to return to the world of mere mortals with their suffering and pain. In this state, your ability to benefit your world is greatly minimized—if you elect to stay, it will mean you have accomplished the quest for spiritually selfish purposes, and though not inherently evil, will have limited your ability to transform the outer world.

Refusal of the return is a rare motif in modern storytelling. Perhaps because of its inverse relationship to the road-of-trials stage and because the road of trials is such a focal point for our societies' current storytelling, it has little use to the modern tale. We can see it, sometimes, in Frodo's sudden desire to take the ring for himself. Having arrived at the summit of Mount Doom and survived so very long, now he wishes to keep the ring and use it for his own power. The refusal finds more of a place in the tales of saints who died in the midst of their ecstasy or in the Buddhist monks who find nirvana, never to return.

Why Refuse?

At the beginning of this section of the journey, we have achieved full realization in the paradise of the gods, the inner world. At our fingertips is the ineffable eternal bliss. To remain in that paradise, to embrace as permanent that gift of the gods that was meant for humanity, this is the refusal of the return.

However, the entire purpose of the quest was not for you alone to transform—it was for the world to transform with you. You become the hero, in the eyes of the world, not when you atone with the father or take the ultimate boon from the gods but when you re-emerge and use those gifts to vanquish the enemies society could not previously without your help.

The purpose of your journey was to give you the insight and realization to change reality. To return to the world changed and to bring your transformation with you. And though the forces of heaven do not seem to state outright that to remain is to fail, it is clear that it is far better to return to the normal world with your gift in hand, prepared to share it with all.

The refusal of the return is tempting for several reasons. One, having tasted the bliss and eternal peace in the abode of heaven, a hero may not ever want to leave. The second problem, however, is that inherent in the return is the fact that the world has not changed along with you.

By this point, you likely feel like a different sort of person altogether. You have transcended, changed completely, and now, returning to normal life, you may be surprised to find that the people you once knew have stayed just as they were—little has changed. They are still stuck, still the same. While some you may never see again—those minor characters in your own life story—there are others who will long for your return. Your family and dearest friends, your social group and culture. All these need what you have gained, for in a way, you gained it not just for yourself but for them as well.

Staying is stagnation. It does the world little good. Personally, I have seen it in those around me enough to know that it leads nowhere in life except toward a frustration that gnaws at your insides until you are forced to move forward. The work you have done up until this point ought to be applied and transferred to the world around you—the knowledge gained, shared. Remember the grace of the goddess, that giving power of the world, and give away what strength you have gained.

At the end of the day, there will be plenty of time to rest in the enlightened state. Until then, return to the world, and play joyfully in the dream of life.

Experiencing the Second Refusal

The second refusal may express itself as a moment of supernal bliss, which is meant to give the hero strength to fight the battle at hand, but which the hero instead revels in. Caught up in the delight of the supernal ecstasy, it is possible to miss out on the battle that is at hand and be defeated. This may play out if the second refusal expresses itself during the final battle moment.

It may be fleeting, or if the initiate chooses to stay, it could last a lifetime. Although the initiate would die in a state of transcendence, their impact on the world would have been limited and the grace they had gained through the ultimate boon lost to the world. How many saints have lived and experienced states of transcendence who would have ultimately benefited humanity only to die in their hermitage or retreat without ever teaching the children of humanity their gained knowledge?

Do not delight overlong in the state of supernal ecstasy— instead, channel that grace energy into the creation of some masterpiece that will stand the test of time, granting enlightenment to any who may happen across it. You will be able to revisit the rune and receive transcendent grace you may not have previously experienced, even during its creation.

Insurance against the Second Refusal

In preparation for this stage, you will not need to tarry long if you have a clearly defined benefactor of your return. It is not enough to have a clear goal if that goal is entirely selfish. You will find, in that case, that in the inner realms of ecstasy and mystical union, you have suddenly found something altogether more valuable than any material gain, and you will likely choose to stay, despite the possibility of selfish gain.

On the other hand, if you know clearly who it is that you will save by your return, you will be motivated out of compassion to do so. Perhaps your friends, family, or a certain people group will most strongly benefit from your actions. Defining that group now will be invaluable motivation to speed you to success in your journey, especially at that crucial moment when you must decide whether to return to the world of the ordinary.

Remember the call of the universe from the apotheosis stage—you have been given a calling, and the energy of the universe now reaches out for you, not for your own benefit but for the salvation of humanity. It is this divine power that will carry you forward, and the completion of the journey will far surpass in internal fulfillment any pleasure you could hope to receive by staying forever at the right hand of the gods.

Preparation for the Second Refusal

As you set out to complete your quest, know that their will come a time when it may be tempting not to continue to move forward for the pure bliss or grace that you find yourself experiencing at a certain point. The temptation will arise in accordance with your level of preparation for the final outward expression as well as with the degree to which completing your quest will benefit the world you live in.

Start now by thinking about the people who will benefit most from the completion of your quest. If you have not concretely formulated a way in which your victory will help them, do so now. Many stand to gain freedom and life from your victory. The goodness of the world exists in the fact that to better your own life, you must also better the lives of those around you or of society as a whole. What group of people will benefit most from your victory?

Imagine how they will benefit. See them rejoicing, celebrating in the product of your victory. Imagine the ways their lives might be changed or transformed. As your vision clarifies, you will ensure you have exceeding levels of power and momentum to return and move forward on your quest. You will also be more willing to pay the price of the road of trials because you will know just how much the world stands to gain from your victory.

13

MAGIC FLIGHT

Sensing his hidden resolve to the task, the wings sud-
denly rushed in on the hero. At once he was lifted up.
The eyes closed and disappeared, and the hall above
opened to the heavens.

All was rushing flight, the wings carrying the
hero by the grace of the Eternal through the heavens.
Below the temple faded rapidly, replaced by the moun-
tain peaks that rushed past like a harsh quilt. Soon
the mountains were replaced by green hills and then
thick dark forest. The valley of his father's house ap-
peared on the horizon, burning red and dark with
smoke. The village rushed up to him, and he was de-
posited like a gift into the midst of the darkness.

All about smoke clouded his vision, tongues of
flame biting mercilessly at his skin.

I Will Show You The World

Wonder. Excitement. Embracing the return, you will now witness all the universe conspiring to bring you directly to the your final battle mo-ment. You will feel the rush, the energy, the thrill as you seem to be lifted up with ultimate boon in hand and sped miraculously to that field which you have dreamt of for so long.

When a traveler embraces the return, the universe itself once more aids him or her. The magic-flight stage is one in which the universe supernaturally aids us in our return to the precise point to provide the greatest benefit to the world. Having accomplished that total transformation necessary to our world's specific plight, the universe now partners with our mastery to speed us directly to the place where we can be the greatest help. In myth, that place may be the very footstep or doorstep of the villain, who we now are able to defeat through the power we possess.

Examples abound of the magic flight in story. In *Lord of the Rings*, once the ring has finally been destroyed, Frodo and Sam are rescued from the burning Mount Doom by the Mythical Eagles, which have time and again assisted Gandalf and the hobbits. In *Star Wars*, we watch as the *Millennium Falcon* speeds out of the exploding Death Star.

In story, these flight scenes often allow the hero to escape from some destructing realm in which the ultimate boon was hidden. In *Aladdin* the ultimate boon is stolen early on. The Cave of Wonders begins to melt a moment later, however— Abu having touched the forbidden gold. Aladdin is aided by the magic carpet and given magical flight. He doesn't make it out, however, and we see the scene transition to a belly-of-the-whale motif. As visible from the Aladdin tale, these motifs do not always appear in the necessary order prescribed. Additionally, not all motifs appear in all stories.

Is It Real?
In life, one of the great mysteries is the method and limitations of magic and miracles. While many aspects of what is

typically thought of as magic are known by modern science to be simply impossible without the assistance of advanced technology, there remains a realm of the miraculous accessible by the modern saint or mystic. Although these miraculous aids fall far short of the magic of many myths, they do exist and can aid the hero in the realm of the real.

In this motif of the magic flight the universe itself will conspire to assist the hero back into the real world, where he is deposited in just the location where he can do the most good. When we think about this happening in real life, we may need some help making sense of it. How could something like this really happen? Rather than write it off as simply impossible, which is what we so often do with fairy tale and myth, lets investigate a bit.

C.G. Jung developed an idea known as the collective unconscious. While Jung's analytical psychology is not typically embraced by the modern professional, his ideas speak to the magic and wonder that really does exist in this world. His idea was that there exists some connected, deep consciousness between us all—and that it is from this collective unconsciousness that our common cultural perspectives and connectedness come from. In the magic flight, it is the power of the collective unconscious that draws the world together.

Just as you have achieved your ultimate boon and made up your mind to use it for the world—then as if miraculously someone will appear on your doorstep, with the keys in hand to take you just where you need to go in order to use the gift you created in the confines of your laboratory.

Or, we could think of the Holy Spirit—that mystical force that in Christian thought that weaves miracles and harmony through the world. This Spirit, all knowing and all powerful, moves in the real world to provide a way for you just as you are ready to utilize it.

So, then, the magic flight is very real—or at least it can be, when recognized and embraced. Unlikely that you will be picked up on a flying magic carpet in the world of the real, but very possible indeed that the connections and relationships you need to get where you are going will materialize in your life just as soon as you need them, and often not a moment before.

Take Flight
Magical flight. Sounds amazing. And it is.

In this stage, having taken the ultimate boon and accepted your call back into the world of ordinary life, you will be aided by all the forces of nature to return expediently to that very point where you can do the most good. Often this is depicted in story as the hero acquiring the sudden supernatural ability to fly.

In story these magic-flight scenes take place toward the very end, usually after the destruction of some epic monument. For the purposes of story, this is accurate, as most tales deal with a motif such as atonement with the father as the central element.

In life, however, atonement with the father and other deeply transformative interior experiences are the climax not of life but of the inward work of the soul in preparation for reemergence into society and the world. Having faced down your inner demons, healed from the pain of childhood wounds, and found a sense of connection with the divine or mystical, the real work now begins.

For the hero of the real world, the magic flight (if it happens at all) will not take place after the final battle but before.

The final battle of the soul, of the interior transformation, is what the stories were talking about. The magic flight will aid you in the return to the ordinary world, where your outward final battle still awaits. It is that outward battle that will be the basis of the following chapters.

In life, rarely do we miraculously pick up off the ground and fly through the air wherever we need to go. However, after having passed every internal trial and attained complete mastery of our own lives, success and victory suddenly gush in on us. If an actor, we find ourselves suddenly on stage, promoted to the very central element of the Broadway cast. If an athlete, it now seems nothing can stop our charge toward our sport's or league's championship game. The forces of nature themselves conjoin to position us for our greatest victory.

Let It Come When It Will

Sometimes we idealize the magic-flight stage itself. We long for it, cherish it as if it were something in itself to be grasped. If only I could get into Harvard, we tell ourselves, then life would be perfect. If only I could receive this promotion, then everything would fall into place.

Status itself is cherished, fought for. In the corporation, people fight their way up the ladder, only to find there is always another rung. And if you reach the top too soon, you may as well fall back down. The mistake here is to hold in high esteem what is actually meant to be a channel for life energy to flow.

What purpose is there in being accepted to that Academy of the Arts unless you are truly ready to compete on the stage with the best of them? Why seek a promotion when, having received it, you could do more harm than good to the organization? The central problem here is that we put our identity—our sense of self-worth and accomplishment—in the title or status we are given by society. However, when we are truly ready, all the doors will open. The universe will expediently grant us everything we need to make our dreams come true the moment we have proven ourselves capable of finishing the battle or completing the quest.

It is a waste of energy to seek that promotion or title before you are ready. The universe will fight with all its might to prevent you from destroying yourself in such a way—for if you do happen to arrive at the scene of your final battle before you are ready, only greater death, failure, and defeat await you. Remember, there is an enemy you have come to destroy, and he is out there waiting for any challenger to arise so he might crush him just as soon as he raises his head in dispute of his reign.

As the magic-flight stage represents the first real return, we should not waste our energy trying to go forward before we are ready. The universe will let us know when the time has come, and at that time we will fly with such speed and grace to the battlefield of our destiny that we will need to hold on as tightly as we possibly can so as not to fall off the magic carpet on our way there!

"Buckle Up, It's Going to Be a Bumpy Ride!"

If and when you do arrive at the magic flight, hold on tight! The universe seems to move extraordinarily fast when this phase comes—although at times it may seem slow at coming.

Imagine a dam holding back a great lake. We stand on the other side of the dam, building our raft, making sure our paddle is ready. We are preparing for that dam to burst. The waters and energies of the universe, when unleashed on us, will carry us far and fast ahead in the journey so that at one moment we are sitting in the darkness of our laboratory crafting our ultimate boon and at the next propelled to center stage in life.

Those very same energies, however, could and will destroy anyone not prepared for them sufficiently. That is why they are sometimes long in coming. God himself is the one holding those energies back—it is his hand that prevents them from coming. When the hero is ready, however, when he has checked in with the Great Captain in the Sky, every preparation made, then the hand of the Creator will be removed, and the miraculous energy of the universe unleashed.

When this happens, simply go with the flow. Allow the universe to give you what it will. It will come fast, and you will need to walk through the doors that present themselves to you. You must trust your instinct, and you must know from your vast training and preparation which wave to ride and which rapid to allow to carry you downstream. Death awaits the unprepared. The ride is not without its own treacheries, and you will need to fight hard and fast now to move forward.

You will succeed, however. The universe will not allow you to die, having come this far—that is the very reason it was waiting so long to unleash this flow. There was one last preparation you forgot to make, and it took three weeks for you to remember to make it. You needed to double- and triple-check every belt and harness, needed to ensure the padlocks were in place and you wouldn't lose your gear on the way down.

Finally, however, the magic flight complete, you will arrive at your destination—the battlefield of your destiny and the place where you will complete your quest in life. You will arrive unscathed, poured out on the ground in such a sudden fashion and with such a display of drama that the flight itself will have once again proven—for any who were yet unconvinced—that you truly are the hero come to save the day.

Preparations for Magic Flight
In life, this stage may come so suddenly that you must always be prepared for it. The magic flight is sometimes a tumultuous journey in and of itself, and at its completion you may have found yourself in your own final battle. You should not long for it to come before you are fully prepared. Make a checklist—what aids and assistance will you need to get where you are going? What small details do you need to complete at the last moment before you take flight?

The universe will not allow you to tarry too long at this stage—the hot-air balloon will take off when it is full, whether you are ready or not. As you see everything coming together, keep going. This is the last opportunity for preparation before the public spotlight will be shining on your face.

Do not be timid when the time comes, either. You could truly miss the boat. Step onto that magic carpet when it comes, walk through the open doorway when it arrives, and embrace the opportunity when it is given to you. The universe will give you the grace to make your last-minute adjustments, if the course is truly worthy and the vision complete. However, if you never intend to finish, the opportunity may pass you by.

14

RESCUE FROM WITHOUT

No sooner had his eyes adjusted to the thick smoke, however, than the glint of a steel spear pierced the haze. In a split second, the boy reacted, bringing his sword up to parry the blow. The next moment he downed the first of the mercenaries, but no sooner than the body hit the ground two more were on him in the place of the first.

Long and hard he fought, but the minions of darkness beat him back. With every faceless rider he defeated, two more took the vacant position.

A cut appeared here, a gash there. The hero was being beaten. In desperation, he thought back to his training, the days of surprising peace being tutored at the hands of the wise old monk.

"This is the gift you will need most when the day comes," the old monk once said.

The monk's words rang with insight through the hero's mind, and suddenly he realized what he had to do.

Falling to the ground, a spear raised above his head for the finishing blow, the hero quieted his mind and called all his energy together within himself.

A roar echoed as the spear fell, but just as it was about to impale the hero, a furry shape burst across his vision. The next moment the haze of smoke dispersed, pushed back by a sudden wind. Looking up, the hero saw the form not of a raven but of a huge eagle, head white and wings blackest black, hovering and with each flap of its great wings beating back the smoke.

Rising from the ground, the hero looked to see a giant grizzly bear now atop the faceless rider. The smoke was clearing, countless eagles fighting it back with wings of might. Across the battlefield, a stag could be seen fighting with antlers bared, lion and serpent now striking out with precision at their common foe.

It was as if all the forces of nature had come together to assist the hero toward his end.

The Battle Commences

Arriving at the doorstep of your destiny, suddenly all the forces of darkness will gush out of the woodwork, trying to beat you back. They may be so overwhelming, in fact, that they overtake you and seem ready to land the finishing blow. Now is the moment you must awaken your spirit, make a call for justice, or appeal to the universal forces of good, nature, or society.

Having come so far, the forces of good will not allow you to be destroyed by the onslaught of evil. Rather, they will rush in to save you, so that you in turn may save them from the evil tyrant you have come to destroy. When your dream is on the doorstep of manifesting, the fight for your destiny will become most apparent. In that moment you must call out, and fight on with ever greater strength, believing in the goodness of the world and leaning on the world's help to save you in your moment of need.

This variation of the return will exist only when your journey pits you against an enemy far too grand for one man or woman alone to conquer. It often expresses itself as a moment of near defeat in the face of an immeasurably strong foe. In this case, even your countless trials and training sessions will not enough for you to singlehandedly defeat the hordes of darkness. The universe, however, will allow you to fail after coming so far.

In story, we sometimes see the rescue from without in a scene where all the allies and friends of the hero must help him in his final battle. For example, in *Avatar*, all the creatures of Pandora are summoned to assist in the final battle. Without their help, the hero and his allies would have been destroyed by the onslaught of massive mechanical weaponry. They help him by removing the preliminary foes who block his path toward his ultimate victory. And in return for rescuing him from a horde far too great for him alone, he defeats that final villain far too powerful for nature itself to destroy.

The Ultimate Symbiosis

The reason the entire world conspires to help you in these cases is clear: through your personal achievement or skill, you can accomplish some task or defeat some great enemy no other soul can overcome.

The world typically does this when you have chosen for yourself some enemy of humanity or good that towers above the entire race, species, or people group. In this case, your arch enemy will have a horde of minions far beyond the number you can deal with personally.

Think of some great social cause—for example, stopping human trafficking. As evil as trafficking is, it continues to plague humanity because of the vast number of human souls who help it. Whether or not there are a few evil overlords in charge of the whole scheme, it is unarguable that there are countless other minions who help it thrive day in, day out. In such a case, a single human can do little to put an end to it.

However, because of the clear evil that it is, the entire world may be convinced to aid such a hero if one could emerge capable of landing the finishing blow. This is the rescue from without.

Against a harsh and evil dictator, the forces of nature themselves await only a hero proven capable of bringing destruction to the tyrant. Faith is required to believe that this is possible—which is why the fundamental inner transformations covered in the second section of this journey are indispensable in such a quest. You must have mastered not just the physical skills required by the road of trials but in this case must undoubtedly have come to some mystical state of union in which you are capable of supernaturally calling on the aid of the entire world—at least the entire world of good or light powers.

It is for this reason we often see characters in reality who seem to be saints but who are, in fact, warriors of social justice. Gandhi, Martin Luther King Jr., Mother Teresa, the Dalai Lama. These are spiritual leaders who took up the call for social justice. Saints and mystics, they represent the completion of the heroic journey in this regard. Their mastery of the supernatural realms of influence allow them to achieve victories for society otherwise unattainable.

After Coming So Far, Do Not Surrender
If the day comes when you find yourself facing down opposition and setback at every turn, especially if it comes when you thought you were so close to the completion of your journey, take heart. Know that indeed, this is just another one of the stages on the journey. Inwardly, congratulate yourself for coming so far. In the next breath, call upon whatever forces of supernatural good or real assistance you can think of. Today, you will need them.

The rescue-from-without motif is another one of those motifs that does not always occur. However, when it does occur, know that it does so because you are oh-so-close to achieving victory in life. Darkness itself, sensing that it is soon to be banished in some great way from not only your personal world, but also the personal worlds of the many you will impact and influence, will now throw every tool and snare it can in your way, in hopes it may overcome you and prevent you from succeeding in your quest.

And know to that the collective powers of darkness may still be beyond your ability to defeat singlehandedly. You are prepared for your personal final battle. You are ready to succeed where all before you have failed. However, you are not alone, and if the entire weight of the kingdom of darkness is thrown in your path, you will need help getting to your final battle moment.

Do not give up hope. Having come this far, you must press forward. And not only that, but you must ask for aid and assistance from the world around you. Whether you do this spiritually or through an actual outward request for assistance will be up to you. It will depend on the specifics of your quest.

Consider the scale and scope of your quest. Is there some cosmic force of evil that will be dethroned by your victory? If so, rest assured that all the forces of hell will stand in your way to prevent you from reaching your goal. Do not be dismayed, however. This simply means that in order to accomplish your goal, you will need to rely on all the powers of good to reach your final battle.

Know, too, that the mystical states of union—meeting with the goddess, atonement with the father, apotheosis, and the ultimate boon—are all the more necessary. You will need not only skill but divine power to accomplish your goal and ensure that the universe helps you along.

It will not be an easy path, but at least you know upfront what will be required of you.

Preparing for the Rescue from Without
Think about your ultimate goal. How grand is its scope? As you start out, if you know how many lives will be changed by your victory or how great the oppression is you seek to displace in the world, you will also be able to measure the resistance the forces of opposition will direct your way when the day comes. The darkness will not be defeated without a fight, and if your quest will free countless lives, you can be sure that it will also ruffle more than a few feathers.

Knowing the scope of the battle, you can know in advance, too, how many allies you will need. You may need only a few, or you may need an entire generation to rise up alongside you to complete your quest. Think about that day—the day the tyranny is destroyed. What will it look like? How many people will participate in your final battle?

If it is more than a handful, know that you will need to become a leader of great import. You will need to rally those who are stuck in bondage and oppression to your call, to convince them to join your fight. Your leadership will display to them that you have what it takes to finish this thing off once and for all—and for that, when they believe in you, they will follow you.

You will also need, at your right hand, allies who possess specific skills you may lack. If you know when that day comes there will be a showdown in an arena in which you are not excellent, you will need to gather at least one good ally capable of seeing that aspect of the quest through on your behalf.

For that person, it will be the completion of a grand quest of his or her own. That battle will make him or her a hero as well, and in the days to come, you will stand side-by-side as victors. With that in mind, think of the skills your allies will need to possess to complement you, and begin to gather them around you now. Share your quest with them, as long as they can be trusted to aid you and not betray you, and breathe the heroic life into them as well as yourself.

Finally, if you truly believe the completion of your quest will result in worldwide freedom from oppression for a specific group of people, take note of it now. You will need to find a measure of faith within yourself to believe the world will aid you when the time comes.

15

THE CROSSING OF THE RETURN THRESHOLD

Standing on the open battleground, minions of the Mascarean Empire falling left and right to the animal guardians of nature, the field seemed to open across from the hero, where there stood a knight in dark mail, a head and a half taller than any normal man. He held in his hand a sword equal in length to a full grown man, formed with black spikes protruding from either side of the blade.

In the distance, beyond the dark lord, the hero noticed his old house—the house of his father. As he watched, the doors opened, and from within emerged his father, followed close behind by his mother.

"Son!" she cried. "You've returned!"

A tear glistening in her eye, she made as if to run toward the boy, but the his father held her back.

"Not yet, Melissa," he said. "We must let him fulfill his destiny."

Father standing with Mother in his arms, the two looked past the dark lord to the boy become man, become hero incarnate. Father nodded, and Mother smiled hopefully, her face suddenly reminiscent of the girl the hero had met in the temple.

Remembering the girl's gentle embrace, the hero now turned to the dark lord. He would do what he had come so far to do.

Locked and Loaded

Having journeyed so far, having died to the world and maybe even literally died once or twice along the way, we now resurrect to the world of the real in the crossing-of-the-return-threshold stage. At this stage in the journey, we fully embrace our real world, reengaging with traditional life and applying that transformation or realization we have gained to the world around us. This is the stage in which we resurrect to the world—where we reengage in that form of life in which we lived prior to leaving and descending into the inner world of personal transformation.

When you are ready, you will step onto the stage in life. At that moment you will reengage with the world you once knew. Your family, your friends will now see you riding through the sky. They will recognize how far you have come, how much you have grown. And in that day, they will see you for the hero that you are.

Remember, as you learned in the chapter on atonement, so often the central reason for your quest is the failing of your society or culture in which you were brought up. Then, when you re-engage with the world and cross the return threshold, the world in which you were brought up will realize that you have purchased for it the cure for its illness.

In their eyes, you will become the hero you set out to be. The quest may not be over yet, but this is a moment of acceptance, of trust, and of hope. Your family and friends, the ones who once thought you lost entirely, will welcome your return, knowing it signals their own freedom as well as yours.

Stride forward confidently when that time comes.

Rolling the Stone Away

This stage is also often signified by an actual resurrection. When the villain, in the final battle, kills the hero outright, then many stages take place all at once—an atonement with the father, apotheosis, meeting with the goddess, or ultimate boon takes place directly after the moment of the hero's death, and having received that reward that only a sacrificial death could buy, the hero resurrects with the ultimate boon in hand, ready to defeat the villain who thought him slain.

This moment in story may come in various forms, depending on what type of story is being told. In simpler tales that deal specifically with those internal workings such as atonement with the father, the motif of crossing of the return threshold and the following two motifs, mastery of the two worlds and freedom to live, can sometimes be minimalized. This is the case in many magical stories.

Because of the emphasis placed by story, especially epic or magical stories, on the hidden or inner world, the return stages become less important. As audiences, we are often captivated by such tales because they are so mysterious to us. We yearn for deeper understanding of them and, especially as youth, desire to grasp them. The more base, boring applications that follow in the return can be put off to an older audience, forced to deal with the ramifications of real life and provision for self and family.

However, these aspects of the return are no less spiritual (in that the mastered spirit must be now applied to reality) or heroic (for they are the realm of the real conflict, the place where adults do battle on the landscape of reality). For the child, who is not ready to be resurrected to the ramifications of adult life, the crossing of the return threshold and the two stages that follow it are simplified or put off entirely.

On the other hand, superhero movies often feature a quick return moment wherein the hero resurrects from literal death with the power to defeat his or her arch nemesis, the supervillain. In myth and religion, Jesus Christ clearly typifies the crossing of the return threshold in his resurrection from the grave.

Embracing the Moment
In life, crossing the return threshold is that moment when the actor or actress emerges onto center stage and can begin the play. Aided by the forces of nature in the magic flight or rescue from without, the spotlight is now focused dead center on the hero. The play has begun, the final game commenced, the battle started, and the hero now has the opportunity to display all those skills and supernatural abilities he has gained along the way.

There is a distinction here between the crossing of the return threshold, which is more a moment in time than other stages, and the master-of-the-two-worlds stage. If the crossing-of-the-return-threshold stage is the actor taking the stage, then the master of the two worlds, which we will cover next, is the act of speaking the lines and awing the audience.

Crossing of the return threshold is the act of resurrection. It is the embodiment of the return and the moment of recognition in the eyes of those watching (whoever they are in your own personal story). The stage that follows will be the proof of what has been gained by the hero's crossover from life to death and back again.

In the quiet place of our practice, we have so fully honed our craft and overcome every internal struggle and battle until we have become of single focus on our goal. Now we have the shining moment and chance to reveal to the world what wonders we achieved.

In story, this is the moment of stepping into battle with the greatest adversary, the villain or arch nemesis who stood so mightily in the hero's way. For an athlete, it may incarnate in taking the field at the beginning of the championship game. For you, whatever your quest or craft or art or trade, it is the stunning moment in which the world receives a vision of your inner mastery through an external display of skill and talent. For the hero, it is that moment in which, having returned from a near- or total-death experience, he now takes up his sword once more to destroy the great villain whom he previously lacked any power to damage at all.

Preparing for the Return Threshold
Once you have come so far, you may feel butterflies in your stomach—or terror if you are facing down some truly evil foe. However, you will also experience the rush of divine energy and the empowerment of knowing you have completed all the stages preceding. The internal transformations of your heart and soul now being complete, you have incarnated the energy

necessary to tear down the giants of the past and erect monuments of victory for the future.

This is your moment to shine, your moment to proclaim your destiny to the terror of the night if necessary or to take the stage as a star burning bright. Run through your accomplishments in your mind briefly. Take note of everything you have learned. When you take this stage, when you step into your own final battle moment, you will need, in the flash of an eye, to express suddenly and dynamically every single stage all at once, one after another in quick succession.

Hopefully by now in reading this book, you are starting to grasp the value of all the preceding stages. You are grasping the necessity to tighten down the hatches here and there in your areas of weakness, in preparation for that one great showdown. As we will see in the next chapter, there has been purpose in it all. Every stage, mastered individually, will suddenly collide into one triumphant moment in your final battle experience.

Standing on the doorstep of your destiny, then, and knowing that you are ready, step out onto the stage and shine like never before.

16

MASTER OF THE TWO WORLDS

Stepping over burning embers, the hero approached the dark lord.

In similar fashion, the dark lord turned to address the hero as he emerged onto the battlefield.

"Do not think with your animal tricks you will defeat me, boy!" the dark lord's voice thundered.

Flames appeared as if to escape the dark lord's visor, and the hero was not sure whether what stood before him was man or deity. It did not matter either way, however, to the hero.

Now standing on the field of battle, the hero remembered his inner vow, and at once the strength gained within the cloister returned like a flash to his being. At first a subtle current, then a roar. Energy began to flow from his heart, from his being. All around the pebbles shook on the ground; the air itself seemed now to swirl around the hero, even as he stood.

He was the light of the world. He was the energy of all infinity, bound to destroy the darkness without.

"Hah!" The dark lord laughed. "Didn't I already tell you that you won't impress me with your tricks, boy?"

The next moment, however, the hero disappeared from the battlefield entirely.

With a flash of lightning from the heavens and a burst of energy before the dark lord, the hero reappeared instantly, sword now buried deep within the dark lord's chest.

With a roar the lord reacted, bringing up his great sword toward the hero. Another flash of blazing light, and the hero disappeared again, only to appear at the edge of the field, far beyond the dark lord's reach.

"I am the light of heaven!" the hero cried. "I am the incarnation of everything that is good and true. And I have come to destroy you!"

Before the dark lord could speak, again the battlefield flashed with lightning. The hero now reappeared beyond the dark lord, standing face-to-face with his parents.

Behind him, a sliver of blood appeared on the neck of the dark lord, and with a gasp, head detached from body, and both fell to the ground, defeated by the boy become hero.

Ascend the Throne

This is the moment you have been waiting for. It is the culmination of your journey—if you dreamt of being or doing something, now is the moment that something will happen. Welcome to your final battle. Welcome to the fulfilment of your call. Here you will accomplish your destiny. Here you will achieve victory in life.

But make no mistake—if getting to this place was a difficult journey, this final battle moment will be the summation of every difficulty so far. This stage, this final battle, is called master of the two worlds for a reason. In this cataclysmic battle, the hero displays full mastery over both self and world. In it, you will be called on to display your own internal and external mastery to the world.

At the beginning of the journey, you set out to accomplish something great. In the second act, the middle section, you mastered your internal world and self. Now, in the third act, you manifest that mastery into the external world. And in this final battle moment, you put on full display both internal and external masteries.

Once you complete this stage, the people of your world, your family and friends, will see you as the hero you have become. Within, however, you will know that you are much more than just a hero. You are a master of the two worlds.

This is the grand finale, that final summation of your skills, gifts, strengths, transformations, and masteries. It is the moment when you put on full display every ounce of skill and strength you have gained along the way. And more importantly, it is that moment when the arch enemy is destroyed; the power that mortal man found impossible to defeat is at last dispatched from the world.

The Microcosm within the Macrocosm

The final battle is the most difficult stage of all. It is the moment you have been building up to, the victory so many have attempted but failed to clinch. The giant you have chosen to defeat has slain all who preceded you, or he would not be alive. During this final battle, you will face not just a new enemy but the summation of every enemy you have defeated so far. The purpose of the stages of the journey was this: that each stage, individually, comprised one fundamental aspect of the grand challenge you set out originally to complete. In that final moment, you will experience every single stage of the journey and have only a heartbeat to express mastery over it before moving on to the next.

The final battle will play out like this:

The call to adventure will be the moment the final battle begins. The refusal of the call will be that voice of doubt that arises for a brief moment, making you wonder whether you can win. Supernatural aid will be a word of encouragement, a smile, or a helping hand from a friend during the fight. Crossing the first threshold will be stepping onto the stage and commencing the battle. The belly of the whale will be a moment you seem to have lost but that you still prevail.

The road of trials will be every parry and thrust, every dodge or act or move while you are on the floor competing for the championship. The meeting with the goddess will be the internal strength to carry on when the fight seems impossible, inspired by the gift you will give to the world. The atonement with the father will be the first strike you land on the opponent to beat him backward, realizing now how far you have come and that you are strong enough to defeat him. Apotheosis will be the energy of the universe rushing out of you supernaturally to carry you to victory. The ultimate boon will be a feat of exceeding grace far beyond the skill of mortals.

The refusal of the return will be the moment you lose yourself to the thrill of the fight, only to realize the enemy has suddenly taken the upper hand and is about to land the killing blow. The magic flight will be the universe rescuing you supernaturally from defeat as soon as you reach out for it. The rescue from without will be the assistance of your teammates and friends in beating the giant back. And the crossing of the return threshold will be the moment you land the finishing strike, defeating that great tyrant you set out long ago to defeat.

At that moment, you will become master of the two worlds. The grand cycle complete, you will have accomplished your destiny—claimed the throne of life and set the world free from tyranny and oppression.

This is the moment you were waiting for, the much-sought-after conquest. Your dream has manifested itself in the world. It is your time to shine and the world's time to rejoice. You have accomplished your destiny, your mission in life is now complete.

There is a central element that begins to culminate at this point. It centers in, focuses. Becomes crystal clear. In hindsight, every stage of the journey takes on significance and meaning; it seems to have a purpose greater than it ever did when the initiate was struggling through on a day-to-day basis. Looking back, you will see how every trial, every twist and turn in the journey prepared you for this fate.

Your day of destiny has arrived. Now the journey completes; now every facet of its pure and perfect form suddenly expresses itself on the stage of life. Victory is achieved.

Reign Free
Master of the two worlds is the total display of mastery gained. Where crossing the return threshold is symbolized by the resurrection itself, master of the two worlds is revealed in deftly landing the killing blow. It is shown, for example, in

Christ as he miraculously appears to the disciples time and again.

When your own personal time to display the mastery you have gained over the world comes, you will be called on to show the fruit of every single one of the preceding stages of the journey. At that time, you will realize that everything you have done up until this point has been nothing but preparation for this one moment, this time that you have been waiting for your entire life.

In the reading of this book, as well, you should note that the form of your own personal final battle—whether displaying some work of art, acting out a play on stage or screen, selling a great work of literature, winning the championship game, or seeing your business explode globally—know that it is this final battle that will define the journey itself.

In order to prove oneself master of both worlds, in this stage the hero must express individual mastery of all the stages preceding. It is only in this grand display of mastery that the arch enemy is defeated and the hero accepted as master of the two worlds.

Armed with that knowledge in advance, you may now find it possible to reverse engineer that journey for yourself. Know simply that the final battle is that place in time where the coalescing forms of all the previous stages of the journey collide to produce some central expression of grandeur and beauty capable of captivating the world entirely.

Preparation for the Master of the Two Worlds
While in the midst of your final battle, there will be little time to think or learn. You must act, you must perform, and you must prove to the world you are ready to become the hero

and master. In advance, however, you can clarify your quest in life and your journey by discerning now what form your final battle will take. What does victory look like for you? What achievement will truly signify that you have accomplished your dream in life?

Is there some specific challenge, for example a championship series or a race, that signifies mastery of your sport? Is there an award to win, such as for an actor or writer? What will be displaced in the world by your victory and accomplishment? Maybe there is some grand enemy, figurative or literal, that you hope to defeat?

Know that the final battle itself encapsulates the entire journey. With your enemy or challenge in mind, think about the journey thus far—how will all the stages cumulate into one grand final expression of inner and outer mastery? At the end of this book, I have included an example journey. That example journey uses the case of a marathon and how this final battle moment may play out during that run. If you need inspiration or understanding, turn to appendix A, called "Example Journey: Getting Healthy," and read through the journey our athlete goes on. Her journey may inspire you and aid you in understanding how your own final battle could unfold.

17

FREEDOM TO LIVE

*In the aftermath of the battle, the villagers began to
stream from their houses. Slowly at first, and then
more and more until they crowded around the hero,
all cheering and congratulating him and longing
just to touch the cloth of his garment. They made to
lift him up on their shoulders, but he bade them stop.
There was one last thing he had to do.*

*Taking the vial of blue liquid from his pocket, he
uncorked it and held it out. Then, turning it upside
down, he poured the brilliant celestial liquid on the
ground. At once, as if by magic—and indeed, it was
the magic of God himself—the earth was renewed.
The smoke cleared, the fire abated, the ground became
green again with grass and leaves, and flowers blos-
somed. The soot disappeared from the face of every
villager, and in that moment the hero turned to his
mom and dad and, with the glisten of a tear on his
cheek, embraced them both.*

*Later, the celebrations of victory finished, the hero
stood beside the grave of his brother and looked down
on the tomb.*

"Never again will brother slay brother," the hero whispered. "I will make sure of it."

The Curtain Falls

Ah, we have finally arrived. The end, the completion of the journey, the last enemy defeated. When you experience this stage, you will be able to relax once more into life, establishing new norms with the progress and change you have accomplished along the way.

I encourage you, however, that this is not the end but the beginning. If you are fortunate enough to reach this stage on your specific journey (not just through reading this book but actually arriving here in real life), then you have likely accomplished some long-held need for change or transformation in your life. As I have said before, so I will say again—Congratulations!

However, there is a vast and beautiful world out there! We have the rest of our lives, and you, reader, may become, over time and journey, a world legend yourself. You may, if you can defeat those dragons and overcome those trials that present themselves along the road, become the hero this world so badly needs. And maybe, just maybe, if enough of us start on this journey together, we can end our time on this planet with a vastly different world than the one into which we were born and give our children the hope of a sparkling and brilliant future, beyond the realms of our comprehension and without the struggles and trials we have met.

Freedom to live is a typical ending in most any tale. In *Lord of the Rings*, we see Frodo, having passed through the shire and dispatched the bandits (master of the two worlds), boarding the ship to the new world. This parallels directly Christ's ascension into heaven, free to live by the right hand of the Father.

In many stories, the imagery ends with a happily ever after. We see the hero, with all his friends and family gathered around, with their new castle or abode. Reconciliations are made, and the darkness the villain brought is at last dispelled. The world returns to peace, and the story ends.

The Goal Attained

Freedom to live is essentially what we start the quest for. It is the final goal, after the final battle, the answer to the frustrations of regular life and the resolution of whatever internal or external conflict held us back in the first place. It is the life you earn by living your dream.

When we enter the freedom-to-live stage, we are already a world-renowned hero. We have whatever it is we need, are more than wealthy enough to survive—although wealth was never really the goal, it somehow always manifests itself to the accomplished hero, who doesn't really need it anyway. And more importantly, by now we will have friends and allies to last a lifetime.

In the freedom-to-live stage, there is a sense of inner peace that transcends all outward accomplishments and need. The hero, task now complete, knows he has accomplished his quest in life. Within himself, it no longer matters how the outward world appears—for he has defeated every great foe along the way and has ascended to the rank of master of the two worlds. For him, he may live in harmony with the world, knowing that when challenge or trial once again arises—and be sure, as long as we live, some trial will find its way to our doorstep—he will swiftly and with great courage and tenacity rise once more victorious in life.

The hero who arrives at this stage has completed the grand journey. He has mastered every single element of a successful human life both individually and in the previous stage, all at once. There is no feat that is beyond his power to achieve—as long as it is in line with his personal calling and quest in life. He may never be an astronaut, but only because an astronaut he is not called to be. Instead, for all his days, he will be a grand personification of the quest to which he was called.

The freedom-to-live stage is not necessarily the end—although it one day will be for you and me. As is discussed in the conclusion, if we arrive here early on in life, we may find ourselves called out once again into the next grand adventure, which may prove to be even better and more miraculous than the first.

There seems to be not much to add here; indeed, it is often nothing more than a wisp in story, a single chapter that provides some sense of conclusion to the whole. In life, however, we often find that the end is nothing but the beginning of a grand new adventure, a journey into the new world.

The final moment, the grand freedom to live, expresses itself in the last breath of life before we venture out to the great beyond—to the next world, whatever it may hold. For the true initiate, the true hero or master of the two worlds, in the words of Albus Dumbledore, "death is but the next great adventure."

Make the Vision Clear
Freedom to live, being the end, is also really the beginning. What motivated you originally to begin your quest? What kind of peace is lacking in your world? If you have trouble defining any of the stages along the hero's journey personally,

think about your desired outcome. What in your life is preventing that outcome from happening? Now work backward through the chapters, answering the exercise questions until you arrive at the beginning. Doing so, you will find yourself more than ready to start out on the grand quest. At that point, finally, you can put this book down (although, like any map, you may need to pick it up again at various points along the way, to remember which direction you ought to go and when) and begin your quest in earnest.

This stage represents the winding down of the story. After defeating the antagonist, arch enemy, or villain, the hero basks in the reward of his victory, not just material but social and psychological—his society accepts and acknowledges him as hero and potentially savior. While there may be monetary gain, usually it is far overshadowed by the true reward of reconciliation with friends and family and the peace gained by returning the world to a state of happiness. A new status quo is set—a happier, more peaceful status quo, with the great villain defeated.

The world can now live in peace. What is more, with the skills and abilities—the profound mastery of self—the hero has gained, money seems a small thing. It comes and goes, but the hero has little need of it. He is the master of both his inner and outer world and is not limited by the mere financial status of his life. Instead, he passes through the halls of leadership and heroism, looked on by all who are good with favor and all who are evil with fear and loathing.

In "Master of the Two Worlds," you were able to clearly visualize what form your final battle would take. Now, in "Freedom to Live," you must define not the battle but the enemy you hope to defeat. What good will come to the world through your victory? What enemy, likely more symbolic than real, will you overcome? Through its destruction, you will become a gift to the world, a messenger from heaven.

Preparing for Freedom to Live

It seems we have come full circle. When you arrive here, you will be at the conclusion of your own quest. And likely, you will find yourself at the beginnings of another. Though you may now pause for as long as you like—you have earned a break, after all!—you will eventually find a calling to a new adventure on the horizon of life.

Today, in reaching the last chapter of this book, you will likely not have set out very far from the time you picked it up. However, your thoughts and imagination and longings of where you would like to go have no doubt changed and transformed by the contents of the chapters you have read.

Take some time now that you understand the entirety of the journey to envision, either with words or thoughts or even art, what you would like your freedom-to-live stage to look like. What does true freedom currently look like to you? How is it different from your reality today?

This vision is the motivation for starting the quest. It is likely that you began to formulate it from the very first chapter, but now it ought to become crystal clear in all its various forms and functions. If necessary, use this answer to think back through the various stages and reformulate them each accordingly. Although the stages are presented individually for the sake of understanding, they are all interdependent on one another, woven throughout the entire tapestry of life. A change in one often signifies or even demands a change to others.

Here the entire journey suddenly sums itself up into one central vortex—a wormhole, if you will, that allows the initiate to proceed with extraordinary speed and grace along the journey. Everything suddenly makes sense; the challenges and difficulties along the way have meaning and are no longer overwhelming but instead become just the stepping stones to true success. And suddenly, as you begin the journey, you may come to realize the cyclic nature of it all—how it builds on itself and morphs into a beautiful fractal shape ever expressing itself in slightly different and altogether new ways.

CONCLUSION

Congratulations! You have reached the end of the road map. You now know your way to the destination and are hopefully equipped with either the tools or the know-how to find them.

The journey we have discussed has crossed all paths in life—from the setting out and breaking of the norm, to the mastery of physical skill, to the psychological battlefields that often prevent us from attaining success, to the road back and putting those hard-won transformations in place. Along the way I have described mystical states, discussed fundamental and cosmological truths, and ventured to help you attain insight and realization into some of the most fundamental psychological states known to man.

Having reached the end of this book, you may just be starting out on your own journey of transformation. This is not the end, then, but the beginning. Furthermore, as you can see, the path to full realization is not limited to one area of the mind or realization—instead, it represents a full, whole life lived with mastery in every realm and regard.

In the back of this book are several appendixes. For ease of access, I have gathered all the exercise questions into one place. I have also provided a short example of how the hero's journey could play out for an everyday goal ("Example Journey: Getting Healthy"). Finally, I have listed in short form the psychological benefit of successfully completing each individual stage.

The road itself will not lead to overnight success. It is not a quick scheme that will somehow, with the snap of a finger, change your life for the better. Instead, it is an arsenal of tools, techniques, and thought processes, synthesized in one place, that through continued use and understanding may assist you to ever-greater realms of success and victory in life.

My greatest hope in concluding this book is that ten years from now, I may look back at my own life and the lives of those who have read it and see along the way countless successes and victories that grew in the fertile soil of preparation and understanding of the path. Hopefully, in this preparation and understanding will be the key to overcoming many of the obstacles and roadblocks that occur along the way for all of us.

As a final note, I would like to encourage you that this path is not a linear journey. Instead, it is a cycle of human mind and thought that plays out on both a daily and sometimes decade-long timescale, as well as on many scales in between. The psychological states, along with the trials and difficulties, manifest in our daily lives on a regular basis.

At the same time, looking back over the years, we may see woven into the fabric of our lives grand themes, playing out over months or years, in which we were decidedly in one stage or another. All the while we may have thought we were going through the entire journey on an almost-daily basis, but in review we see that the grand cycle has played out only once over the last ten or twenty or thirty years.

I encourage you to understand that this is a natural part of human struggle and existence. Indeed, the myths tell of grand epochs in which one part of the journey alone played itself out for millennia at a time. The old phrase "the microcosm in the macrocosm" holds true, on this battlefield of the mind in which we wage our particular wars.

As you review this work, I hope you take the time to answer the exercise questions at the end of each chapter. Distill for yourself your own particular journey, and then, when all preparations have been made, set out! You may find yourself needing to adjust along the way, as any good journey should have you do, but do not fear! Eventually, you will find yourself at a goal—if not the original one you set out to accomplish, then one much better. Indeed, you may find that the goal you set was accomplished very early on in the journey, and since then you have gone on to achieve much more!

FINAL BENEDICTION

I have a bit of a confession to make. When I started out writing this book, I knew vaguely what form I wanted it to take. I had in my possession *The Hero with a Thousand Faces* and had relied many times before on the hero's journey in crafting fictional tales. I had never, however, fully sat down and applied in such great depth every stage of the journey to a modern life.

I knew intuitively how much value such an undertaking would garner but did not yet hold the specifics of it in my hands. As I worked through the various stages of the journey, I was forced to search within myself and in the writing available to me for deeper meaning, fuller understanding. As I did so, the journey became clearer to me—life started to make more sense.

What had seemed before a confused mess of the different colors of life, beyond all recognition or meaning, suddenly began to reveal a pattern before my eyes. As I wrote and worked on this book, meaning in the smallest details of life became apparent. What is more, those funny little coincidences and circumstances, which before were just that, now told me specifically where I was in the journey.

This book, this road map, is a set of keys to life. If understood and applied, you will gain the power to understand the hidden language of the cosmos—what your external reality is really trying to tell you. And knowing this language, you will be able to speak back to that reality—to communicate with the world through these symbols and meanings. As meaning becomes clearer, the tapestry becomes more defined. Suddenly beautiful pictures emerge where prior there were only muddied vagaries.

And the longer you stay on this journey, I am told, the more grand and incredible it becomes.

I have a vision as I close this book, not of just of one or two souls becoming heroes on the journey of life, but of countless souls accomplishing their dreams and becoming true masters in life. Perhaps, if this were possible, over time a wave of transformation would sweep our society and lives. Together, the effect of a thousand heroes all emerging from the fabric of reality may be the final cosmic push required to utterly transform our society.

I can only wonder and imagine what great dreams or miracles will take place on that day. Freedom, love, and prosperity never before imagined made available to all members of our race. The wonders of the universe may resolve before us, humanity itself at once stepping into a new era of awakening.

APPENDIX A—EXAMPLE JOURNEY

Getting Healthy

Call to Adventure: "I feel so unhealthy. I really should change. I should stop eating so many cookies and use less cream in my coffee."

Refusal of the Call: "But it's *so* hard. I will have to give up my sugar." Eats another cookie.

Supernatural Aid: "No, I really need to do it, and I need to start today! Hooray!"

That same day, finds a workout book perfectly tailored to personal needs.

Belly of the Whale: Starts working out and eating right. Looks in the mirror.

"Whoa! When did I get so fat? I mean, I knew I was unhealthy, but really? Damn!"

Road of Trials: "OK, got to start working out." Goes to gym.

"OK, got to start eating right." Starts diet plan.

Meeting with the Goddess: "Wow, I am starting to look really good. My body feels great. This is awesome."

Woman as Temptress: COOKIE: "You can eat me. After all, look at how *far* you have come! Come on, just one bite!"
PIZZA: "Oh, and a piece of me too!"
HERO: "Never, Cookie! Never, Pizza!"

Atonement with the Father: "Man, I'm starting to look and feel better. It's been about three months. Why don't I just give up?"

"Crap, did I just give up again? What the hell is wrong with me?"

Realizes parents never really forced her to do anything she didn't like for very long—took her out of things before she could get good at them and so on. Forgives parents and learns the hard way.

Apotheosis: "I am the perfection of fitness. I am health itself." Jams to "Eye of the Tiger."

Ultimate Boon: "Seven percent body fat? *I'm gorgeous!*"

Refusal of the Return: "I love the gym. Why don't I just stay here all day long and never do anything else?"

Magical Flight: Sees a small child on the side of the street. Above the child is a poster that reads,

"Freedom to Live Marathon—Run to Benefit Orphans Worldwide."

Heart breaks. "Actually, maybe I'll run a marathon."

Same day, friend says, "Hey, I just signed up for a marathon. Want to join?"

Crossing the Threshold: Day of the marathon arrives. Looks around, sees all the athletic people. Thinks, "Am I really here? Am I really one of them?"

Steps up to the starting line. "Remember, though, this isn't about you. It's about the children."

Master of Two Worlds: The starting shot fires. The runners are away. The hero is away. It's hard, but she keeps up. A cup of water extends from the sidelines, and she takes it. The path curves and rises; still the hero runs. Speeds up. "Why don't you just give up a bit?" Temptation says. Thinks about the children and speeds up some more.

Suddenly, a weight clings to the hero's shoulders, and fatigue sets in. "You have to give up," another voice says, this one far stronger.

"No, the hero responds." Forgives parents. "You taught me to give up before I had achieved victory, but I won't give in. I will finish this race and win!"

Suddenly, the world melts away. Runner's high sets in. The hero has boundless strength. Left and right she passes runners. Left and right they fall away. "You could stay here all day just enjoying the run," a third voice chimes.

The hero looks up. "No, the finish line is in sight. Three more opponents remain."

Breaking from the pack, the hero now sprints. Energy from within propels her ever forward, until at last the ribbon breaks. The crowd cheers. A trophy is forced into her hands. Lights flash. Tears stream down her face.

Freedom to Live: She did it. She won. They congratulate her, ask her how she feels. She utters some words that don't even come close to the overwhelming sensation of victory within. She hardly believes it.

Later, sitting in her home, she takes up some new job and realizes those things that before seemed so difficult in life are now nothing but blips along the way. Challenge no longer defeats her. She is free to live at last.

APPENDIX B—INVENTORY OF GIFTS

1. **Call to adventure**: freedom from boring, average, normal life
2. **Refusal of the Call:** assurance that the task is worthy; inner commitment to the call
3. **Supernatural Aid:** the encouragement and approval of the external world
4. **Crossing the First Threshold**: the knowledge that you are capable of completing the task
5. **Belly of the Whale:** psychological transformation; a new perspective aligned with the truth of reality
6. **Road of Trials:** the concrete skills necessary for success
7. **Meeting with the Goddess:** grace to give and create
8. **Woman as Temptress:** proof that the prize is valuable and worthy of sacrifice
9. **Atonement with the Father**: inner transcendence; mastery of yourself and the world
10. **Apotheosis:** divine insight into the nature of reality
11. **Ultimate Boon:** supernatural ability to perform beyond what is natural or reasonable

12. **Refusal of the Return**: understanding of the value you bring to the world
13. **Magic Flight**: aid of the external world in accomplishing your task
14. **Rescue from Without**: confirmation of the world's desperate need for your achievement
15. **Crossing the Return Threshold**: acknowledgment of internal value in the lives and actions of the external world
16. **Master of the Two Worlds**: external victory, achievement, accomplishment, and success
17. **Freedom to Live**: peace, harmony, fulfillment of having accomplished your personal quest or destiny

APPENDIX C—EXERCISES

Exercises for the Call to Adventure

Make a mental inventory of your life. What do you enjoy? What areas of dissatisfaction come to mind?

It is important for you to understand from the beginning which type of adventure you will have. Will your adventure be one for yourself, or will it be one you undertake for another? (Feel no shame if it is the first—that is just fine!)

Finally, whether you embark on this adventure for yourself or someone else, take the time to define your goal. What do you hope to accomplish? Knowing this will form the basis of your ability to answer all the proceeding exercise questions.

Exercises for the Refusal of the Call

What scares you most about your chosen call?

What could go wrong on your journey?

Are you setting out to do something you have tried to do before and failed? If so, how can you modify your goal to make it more attainable?

Knowing what you know now, how can you overcome the foreseeable difficulties along the way?

Exercises for Supernatural Aid

Have you ever experienced a strange amount of unexpected encouragement from the world around you, encouraging you to continue something you have started?

If you have started and given up, think back to the previous times you started. Was any external aid given to help you? It may not be as magical as in a story. For example, it could be as simple as a stranger's smile at the right moment or a word of wisdom from one wiser than you.

Finally, prepare yourself by knowing that when the time comes to start out, the universe will invariably give you some help along the way.

Exercises for Crossing of the First Threshold

Allow the voices of discouragement to come. Do not balk at their coming. Instead, listen to them. If it helps you, even write their complaints down for reflection.

Having listed the complaints of the inner voices of discouragement, reflect on how you can overcome them. Remember, your mind is simply making you aware of the very real challenges ahead.

Having conquered your internal demons of discouragement and despair, you may be more confident to set out on your own personal quest. However, before you go out and tell people where you are going, I strongly encourage you to read the rest of this book. It is a map, and as a map it will describe to you many more places you will go along your journey. Before setting out, you still ought to know all the stops along the way. You may find that by the time you finish this book, your entire destination has changed, and in that case, you will be very glad to have held off on announcing your intentions to go before you really understood where you were going.

Exercises for the Belly of the Whale
If you do find yourself in this stage, the worst thing you can do is try at once to change everyone around you. Although you may suddenly see in your family everything wrong with the world, it is a mistake to attempt to fix it at this stage. In reality, you see reflected in them all your own personal failings. Take a moment to grieve this passage, and let go of your attachment to how things are. You are just starting out on this journey.

Next, resolve within yourself to change. And having this resolve, step forward into the journey of life. When you conclude this journey, you will be able to return to your family and friends victorious, healed and transformed inwardly, and offer outwardly true change and transformation.

Exercises for the Road of Trials
What form do you suppose your final expression of mastery will take?

In order to achieve such mastery, what individual skills will you need to possess?

Draft a plan to achieve mastery in each of the skills identified above. If you are well along on your journey in life, you may now realize you are lacking in one or two of those required skills. In that case, focus on bringing those skills up to a sufficient level with your plan.

Exercises for Meeting with the Goddess
Take some time to review your own quest goal. Look deeply at your motives. In what ways are they self-serving or self-centered?

Understanding that the sacred marriage with the goddess takes place when a hero chooses to sacrifice himself to save the object of his love, how can you reorder your motivating thought processes to be more focused giving to others?

Exercises for Woman as Temptress

What are your most prevalent personal vices or moral failings? Be sure, as you push forward on your quest, they will raise their ugly heads when you are least ready for them. List them here:

Clearly state the goal of your quest in a single sentence. This goal, clearly defined, will be your focus when temptation arises.

Exercises for Atonement with the Father

In order to find internal peace, we must heal the wounds our fathers inflicted on us in childhood. If you are just starting out, working with a trained counselor may be helpful in this regard.

Forgive your father for any pain he has inflicted on you. As you think about your childhood and images arise, focus on forgiving him and healing from the wounds.

Exercises for Apotheosis

Ask yourself if you are ready to perceive the depths of reality and transcend the limitations of normal human consciousness.

Exercises for the Ultimate Boon

Like other revelations about the spirit and self, the ultimate boon cannot directly be prepared for. Instead, it is the culmination of countless hours of hard work and dedication combined with the psychological readiness that presents itself when the spirit is whole.

The best approach you can take is to visualize yourself completing your chosen craft, trade, or art in the state of "flow." Self-visualization has been proven to be a powerful tool for entering into altered states of consciousness. Take some time to see and feel yourself succeeding or achieving victory in your chosen arena.

If you seek to produce in your quest a magnum opus, what form will it take?

Exercises for the Refusal of the Return
At the completion of your journey, what groups of people will have benefited from your victory? List any groups you can think of.

In what ways will they benefit from your victory?

Exercises for the Magic Flight
In what ways may you need some additional external help when the day for your reemergence comes?

Exercises for the Rescue from Without
Think about your ultimate goal. How grand is its scope?

Will you need allies to assist you in its completion? If so, can you think of what complementary skills they may need to best assist you?

Do you believe the completion of your quest will result in worldwide freedom from oppression for a specific group of people? If so, express it here. Find some measure of faith to believe that the world will aid you when the time comes.

Exercises for the Return Threshold
When you return, what form will your stage take?

Exercises for the Master of the Two Worlds
While becoming master of the two worlds gifts the hero with material rewards, the true reward is victory over the hero's enemy. What grand enemy, figurative or literal, do you hope to defeat?

Know that the final battle itself encapsulates the entire journey. Think about the journey thus far—how will all the stages cumulate into one grand final expression of inner and outer mastery?

Exercises for Freedom to Live
Using words or otherwise, paint a picture of what you want your desired outcome to look like.

How is your desired outcome different from reality today?

What giants or enemies exist in your life today that do not exist in your desired outcome? If necessary, use this answer as a starting point to work backward through the exercises of the hero's journey.

BIBLIOGRAPHY

Campbell, Joseph. The Hero With a Thousand Faces. Princeton, N.J.: Princeton University Press, 1949.

Rowling, J. K., and Mary GrandPré. Harry Potter and the sorcerer's stone. New York: A.A. Levine Books, 1998.

Bible. New King James Version is quoted.

"apotheosis." Merriam-Webster.com. 2017. https://www.merriam-webster.com (23 January 2017).

www.ingramcontent.com/pod-product-compliance
Lightning Source LLC
LaVergne TN
LVHW041252080426
835510LV00009B/701